1 MONTH OF
FREE
READING

at

www.ForgottenBooks.com

By purchasing this book you are eligible for one month membership to ForgottenBooks.com, giving you unlimited access to our entire collection of over 1,000,000 titles via our web site and mobile apps.

To claim your free month visit:
www.forgottenbooks.com/free704107

ISBN 978-0-483-00291-3
PIBN 10704107

THE KINGS

MOST GRACIOUS

MESSAGES FOR PEACE,

AND

A PERSONAL TREATY.

Publifhed for His Peoples Satisfaction,
that ·they may fee and judge, whether
the foundation of the Commons Declaration,
touching their Votes of no farther Addreffe
to the K I N G, (*viz*.His Majefties
averfeneffe to Peace) be juft,
Rationall and Religious.

PSAL. 21. 7.

*The King trufteth in the Lord, and through the
mercy of the moft High he fhall not be moved.*

Printed in the Yeare, 1 6 4 8.

Printed in the Yeare, 1 6 4 8.

TO THE READERS,
of whatsoever Nation, Quality, or Condition.

Readers,

He Papists teach, that Ignorance is the Mother of Devotion; *but we believe, of mischief* rather. The world knew him not, *says the Spirit, of our Saviour, for* had they known, (*as in another place*) they would not have crucified the Lord of Glory: *and of Ignorance it was, they desired* Barabbas, *and denyed* Jesus: I wot that through Ignorance ye did it (*sayes the Apostle.*) *So many people (in these times) have been busily mischievous against their King* through Ignorance, *because they did not know Him:* for had they known *His Vertues and His Graces, they would not (doubtlesse) have opposed Him, nor preferred such (as they have done) before Him.*

But as our Saviour *was; so hath our* Soveraign *been, shaddowed much from vulgar Eyes, by the black cloud of sclaunder and reproaches; which notwithstanding was, and is removed from each, by the patient sufferings, gentle actions, and gracious sayings of them both: so that what*

A 3

was

was hidden, did, and doth (at laſt) appear (maugre ſpight) to admiration. Verily this was the Son of God, *(ſaid ſome of Chriſt in thoſe dayes, who before had thought but meanly of him.)* And againe, Never Man did, or ſpake like him. *So thoſe men, who (when time was) had low opinions of their King, are even forced to confeſſe now, that* Doubtleſſe He is a man of God, highly beloved of the Father, for never any (in the midſt of ſo much ſorrow) ſuffered, acted, or writ better then He hath done.

What Chriſts Minde *and* Spirit *was, (even unto thoſe who ſtudyed His hurt) the Goſpell ſhewes ; and (that all men might know the ſame) 'tis His Command to read that :* Search the Scriptures *(ſayes he)* for they are they which doe teſtifie of me. *Indeed they are* His Meſſages of Peace to mankinde ; *they diſcover His love and diſpoſition to us, His ſtrong deſires of Reconcilſation with us. And of like naïure or kinde to* them, *are theſe enſuing* Royall Papers ; *which (alſo) for a like end, are here collected, publiſhed, and preſented in one view: (that the world might more fully ſee, and know the King.)* They are Meſſages of Peace *from* Him the wronged *party, and may be (not unfitly) called* His Majeſties Goſpell *to His people : wherein they may moſt clearly view His Gracious Spirit, and His temper ; His gentle Nature and diſpoſition, even towards thoſe, who take pains and pleaſure both, to vex and grieve Him.*

Had that Heathen Senate *of old* Rome read *Chriſts* Goſpell, *and Him therein, His power and readineſſe to ſave them, they would not (doubtleſſe) have voted Him* no God : *So it may be thought, if the* Senate *of theſe dayes, had read theſe Meſſages of their Soveraign, with a right Eye ; and obſerved His goodneſſe expreſſed in them, His ability and willingneſs of minde to pardon ſuch as themſelves are : they would not have voted Him* no King, *or (which is little leſſe)*

no

To the Readers.

no more *Addreſſes* to be made to Him. *But (it ſeemes now) through their default in grace and light ; His Majeſties Regality (like Chriſts Divinity) muſt depend upon the approbation of His own Creatures,(for ſuch they are, as they poſſeſſe the place of Senatours;) and muſt paſſe for currant no longer in the world, then they ſhall pleaſe to allow of it.*

But doth not this Act of theirs proclaime to all , they fear not God ? *'tis His command, that if a* Brother, *an equall, or common man* be at odds *with any, there ſhould be a* going or ſending to, *and a* receiving from, *till a concord be concluded: but theſe being at difference with their King , their Soveraign , their Publick Father, (to whom they owe all duty) have voted the quite contrary ; and Reſolv'd upon the Queſtion,* that no more Addreſſes be made unto, or received from Him : *and ſuppoſing that this their oppoſition unto God, might be noted to their ſhame; they have ſince that, adviſed upon an Ordinance* that none ſhall preſume to ſpeak againſt them, *or to finde fault at their ſo doing. This is the Divinity of theſe times, or rather of theſe new Reformers, but we refer their* doings *to the worlds cenſure, and themſelves to the Judge of all fleſh.*

Readers, *You have here ſet before your Eyes, Piety and Conſcience ; Wiſdome and Humility ; Majeſty and Mercy : Bowels of Compaſſion, and Charity to Friends and Enemies : Yea, what ever diſcovers a good King, and a perfect Chriſtian ; you ſhall meet with it in theſe* Meſſages of His Majeſty : *Behold them , Read them , Conſider of them : And let that ſweet* Spirit of God *which ſhines and breathes in them, be conveyed plentifully into your Hearts by them.*

The Preface.

Ad *Solomon* lived in our daies, He would scarce have said, *there is no new thing under the Sun,* or *that which is,hath been,*for surely that which now *is,* hath never *been* : the *Sun* never saw such a *shamelesse* and *viperous* Generation,as the wicked world in this her *last* and *worst* Age hath brought forth ; *Patience* cannot mention them, without a zealous *passion* against them : and should Christ himself speak of them, He would say *they were of their father the Devill,* who undoubtedly hath put forth his whole strength to their begetting, by whose sole help He hopes (under contrary pretences and professions) for ever to disgrace, (if not to ruinate) *Christian verity* in this Kingdome, to banish all *Duty* and *Charity* from among us, to rob us of that *Liberty* which no people like us did injoy, and to keep us under the most *cruell* and *unreasonable* Bondage that ever was, and so to make us (who were the Happiest) of all nations the most *miserable* and *despised.*

To which ungodly ends, this *sinfull Brood* have raised a most wicked war in their own native Country, against their Soveraign, (the indulgent Father of it) unto whom themselves had often sworn *fidelity* and *Allegiance* : nor hath the supream *Moderator* of Heaven and Earth yet stopt them in their way, but (for the due punishment of our sins, the full discovery of their incredible wickednesse, and of those admirable graces in the King) hath suffered them rather to prevail, prosper, and grow worse and worse these 7 years together : in which *interim* or space of time, His

sacred

facred Majefty (though the wronged party) imitating the *Great* and *Good God*, hath often in his Commiferation and pity both to us and them, (of our *mifery* and their *madneffe*) fought Peace at their Hands, who for no caufe had broke the fame ; yea and of-fered more for the Purchafe of it, then was ever till now defired of any Englifh King.

But they defigning (as is now Evident) to inflave us, and fettle themfelves in his Throne, have like *deaf Adders* ftopt their Ears, and been moft perverfe unto all defires of that nature : yea, and to prevent his fending them any more, have now at length not only imprifoned his *facred Perfon*, but alfo (as may be affirmed) *interdicted* him all Humane Society, by voting *no further Addref-fes to be made unto Him*, and forbidding all men, (under penalty of High Treafon) *to receive, or bring any Meffage from Him*, fo tedious (it feems) to the Haters of Peace, are motions there-unto, and fo irkfome is Reafon to them who refolve to Heare none.

But fuppofing in their black Policy, this Height of impiety, might fomewhat Startle the amazed world, who had not been acquain-ted with the like before, they promifed a *fatisfactory Declaration*; wherein fhould be fhewn the Reafons of fo ftrange Votes and courfes ; upon which the feduced part of men grew big with ex-pectation, and looked for fome new *great mountain of Errour* to be brought forth againft the King, never yet feen or heard of : But behold, at laft what appeared ; only a parcell of *ftale ftuffe*, a new Heap of *old tales* without proofs, which had been oftner told and confuted already, then there be *Members* left in both Hou-fes ; fo that the repetition of them on this occafion, is confeffed by thofe who were blind before, to be but an open difcovery of an *impotent fpight* that wants nothing but matter to work upon : And fo far, is this *Declaration* from fatisfying amazed minds, con-cerning thofe uncouth votes, that it rather leaves them more a-ftonifhed, the *Ground* or caufe thereof being more ftrange and im-pudent, then the *votes* themfelves, viz. *the Kings averfneffe unto Peace*, it begins thus :

How fruitleffe our former Addreffes have been to the King, is fo well known to the world, that it may be expected we fhould now de-clare, why we made the laft, or fo many before, rather then why we

are

are resolved to make no more.   And again in the same page,

We have no lesse then 7 times (being never yet forced thereto)made such Applications to the King, and tendred such Propositions, that might occasion the world to judge, we have not only yeilded up our Wills and Affections, but our Reason also and Judgment, for obtaining any true Peace or good Accommodation. But it never yet pleased the King to accept of any tender fit for us to make, nor yet to offer any fit for us to receive.

Had these men who thus speak, acted the Kings part, and He theirs, there might have been much of *truth,* though little of *Piety* and *manners* in these Expressions of their Soveraign : or had Affairs betwixt His Majesty and them been agitated in a Corner, & not in the worlds Eye, perhaps by these so confident aspersions of him, some ill *suspitions* might have risen in peoples minds against him ; but the case being as it is, and matters been acted as they have, on the publick Stage, we have cause to admire at their Hard foreheads. Certainly did they not fancy us stark blind, they would not tell us it were night at noone day : did they not think us given up to the strongest delusions that ever were, they would not speak to us after this fashion : but from this their *Language,* we shall learn this *Lesson,* That *they who are not ashamed publickly to Charge such a thing upon their King, so manifestly contrary to all mens knowledge, will never blush to traduce him to the full Height, in matters more secret, or lesse visible.* This beginning of their *Declaration* (therefore) doth well instruct all people, how to believe them in the sequel of it.

These Brass-brow'd and unreverend Men, that so boldly affirm *the world well knows how fruitlesse their former Addresses have been, &c.* cannot shew one *Addresse* so qualified as they speak, ever made by them to the King, that proved *fruitlesse :* they cannot name any one *Act,* wherein they denied their own *Wills,* or discovered the least good *Affection* to their Soveraign, since the beginning of these Divisions ; nor can they instance in any one *motion* ever proceeding from them unto His Majesty, and refused by Him, that had any favour of right *Reason,* or relish of true *Judgment* in it : nay, have not themselves continually slighted,and most unreverendly rejected what ever Messages of that nature have been sent from him ? did His Majesty ever demand any thing of them, that was not His own by *Law*? nay, in order to Peace, did He ever ask so much as by *Law* was due unto Him? did He not alwaies recede from the same, to satisfie them, if their guilt and perverseness had not made them uncapable of Satisfaction? Surely the King hath not 7 times onely, but rather 7 times seven within these 7 years, made such *Applications* to them, offered such *tenders* of mercy & pardon, and of His own undoubted Rights & Priviledges, as did (in very deed) occasion the world to judge, that He had *yeilded up His will and Affections*, yea *His Reason, Judgment, and all, for the obtaining of a good Accommodation :* but they would never yet please to accept of any ; when He spake to them of *Peace*, they Hardened their Hearts against it, and made themselves *ready to Battaile :* these things they know we are able to demonstrate, being such as the *world* hath taken full notice of ; and yet with what audaciousnesse doe they affirm the Contrary before the *worlds* face, to the Kings dishonour, and their owne Commendation, (as they would have it ?)But(it seems) Change is no Robbery in their opinions ; sith they return to the King what is theirs, and apply unto Him their own Conditions, in lieu of that Candour and righteousnesse which they take from Him, to paint themselves withall, they think they have done very good Justice. Our Saviour Himself had to doe with such persons, who could charge him home with their own faults, and appropriate most favourably to themselves, that Innocency and goodnesse which was truly His ; they could accuse and sclaunder His Holy Actions, and give a large good report of their own ill doings, whereby (as He saies) they spake their *Testimony* to be *untrue*, and themselves *Children of the Father of Lies :* so whosoever considers what these have writ must needs conclude the like of them, *even that Satan is in them of a truth.*

But their Conceit (as appears) is, that the last word will get the day, and credit enough to their sayings, and this they think they are sure of ; for 'tis fore-provided that His Majesty shall either not know, what they object, or if He doth, and hath a mind to speak for Himself, He shall not be suffered ; nor must any man dare (under pain of *High Treason*) to bring from Him into publick view any *Papers* or *Writings* of what kind soever, though tending only to the vindication of Himself from their base, vile,

and

and ungodly sclaunders ; it must be sufficient to condemn Him, that they who thirst for His bloud have thus accused Him. And here is the *wisdome* of these Happy times, this is the *Justice* of our blessed Reformers. Sure had they any Hope that the King were likely by impertinent discourses, to Help their lame and barren cause with some advantages, they would easily admit of a *Treaty* with Him, (what ere they say to the Contrary :) or did they imagine His Royall Pen could speak any thing but *Innocency,truth,* and *Reason,* they would be content to hear from it, upon this their further provocation of it : but wholly despairing of such matters, they have thought meet, to imprison both Him and His Pen too, which (they know) would in a moment cast down this idle *Cobweb,* as it formerly hath done others of like nature, and they think to stop all mens mouths, by affirming *the world well knows How fruitlesse their former Addresses have been to the King.*

But though His Majesties Hands are thus tied; this *Spiders web* must not scape brushing : before it had Hung 3 daies, an Honest *broome* reached at it, a wholesome *Antidote* came out against it; and made it appeare to be as it is, fit onely for the draught or Dunghill ; and almost daily since, some Loyall foot or other, hath been trampling on it : for *Stones* would surely *move,* and stir in this case, if men should not.

But sith none can speak so well as the King, and He is *voted* to speak no more, and sith their *appeal* is made to the *worlds* knowledge, it shall not be amisse, for the *world* to look back upon what the King hath said or done already, even in Confutation of that here Charged upon Him, scil. *His aversnesse unto Peace :.* perhaps thereby alone, it will sufficiently appeare, that of all sclaunderers which ever were, these *Declarers* have deserved the name of the *most impudent,* and *most shamelesse.*

We shall not need to look back so far as to the years 1642. & 43. or call to mind His Majesties unwillingnesse to war at first, His many Messages to prevent the same, and to preserve peace, before it was broken ; or to mention how *scornfully* they were entertained, as effects only of His weaknes,& instances of His want of power to make resistance. Nor will we remember how by force of Arms, they had kept him out of His town of *Hull,* taken His *Militia* and *Navy* from Him, and raised an *Army* against

Him,

Him, before He set up His *Standerd* in His own defence against
them (which His desire of Peace had prevailed with him to take
down again, and to recall his most just *Declaration*, so that their
unreverend and scandalous *Libels* against him might but likewise

he Earles of
orset and
outhampton.

be recalled :) nor yet how in those daies his Messengers, men of
High Nobility and great Honour (against whom they had nothing
to object but that imployment) were not suffered in person to declare their Message, (because it was *for Peace*) but commanded to
depart the town speedily. Nor how at other times they imprisoned others that came to them on the same Errand, how they
often neglected to return Him any *Answer* at all, or perhaps in
lieu thereof (after a moneths delay) they would send Him a parcell of reproachfull expressions, and peevish constructions of
what He had writ in the sincerity of His heart, and pity of Spirit
for the insuing Miseries of His people ; which notwithstanding
He would still interpret, and call, but *mistakes*, that He might not
exasperate (if possible) their ulcerated minds unto contention,
though in very deed, they were no other then High Sclaunders
& studied Contempts. Nor wil we call to mind how once in particular His earnest pressing for *peace* by a second and third *Message*, (before He had received Answer to a former,) did appear
so intolerably offensive unto them, that to teach Him to make an
end of such motions, and to prevent (if it might be) all further
molestations from Him of that nature, they fell the very next day
(after their receipt thereof, having first committed His Messen-
ger) to accuse His Majesties *Royall Consort* of High Treason.
But these things at so large a distance we need not remember ;
nor how his Majesty after the often frustration of such His own
endevours for *Peace*, did convene the loyall Lords and Commons
at *Oxford*, to consult of a way to procure that desired blessing ;
how they laboured in vain about the same, and had their Letters
which they sent to that end cryed up and down *London streets* in
scorn, under the Title of *a Petition of the Prince of* Wales, *and
Duke of* Yorke *for Peace.* How in answer thereto, Papers full of
Treason, sedition, and disloyalty were sent unto them, together
with that unlawfull *Covenant* (which now themselves deride at,
as an *Almanacke of last year*, or occasionall trick devised at the
present to cheat the Kingdome) for His Majesty and all in *Ox-*
ford

ford to take : nor need we remember how all thofe Noble and Loyall men did under their Hands atteft (to all the world) His Majefties earneft longings to have a period put to thefe unkind divifions, which Himfelf alfo by his Actions did alwaies confirm, whofe conftant courfe it was, at the end of any *Victory* got by him, or any remarkable *defeat* given to them, to fend forth His Proclamations of Mercy and tenders of pardon (which are ftill extant in many hands) on Condition they would but. at length be quiet and imbrace *peace*, which they would never confent unto, unleffe He would alfo yeild to Juftifie their *Jealoufies*, and to condemn Himfelf as guilty of all they had Charged upon Him : And 'tis well enough known that when ever He procured to have a *Treaty* with them (which was but feldome) His *Propofitions* were fo much tending to their *advantage*, and his owne *damage*, that nothing difliked them more, then His *moderation*, which indeed was the true caufe of their continuall backwardneffe unto *Treaties*, and alfo of their ftrict *Limitations* to their Commiffioners, when with much adoe they were obtained, (as is evident enough by the paffages of that at *Uxbridge* :) for they fuppofing the *reafonableneffe* of what they knew His Majefty defired, and the *unreafonableneffe* of what themfelves intended to aske, would be fo apparent by a free and open difcuffion, that a Peace thereby might happily be produced in defpight of them : wherefore their care was to prevent (if they could) any *Treaties* at all, or elfe by devifes to break them off, before they came to any perfection; and then they would with all fpeed make a *Declaration* to the world, wherein they would pretend fully to fhew, that *His Majefties demands had neither Reafon nor Juftice, either in the matter or manner of them, but were fuch as left the people no Hopes to fee an End of their prefent Calamities.*

But (as was faid) we fhall not need to look back fo far for Helps to overthrow the Groundwork of this their falfe building; we fhall onely remember the meanes ufed by His Majefty for *Peace*, fince His peoples Calamities are confeffed without difpute, to be folely continued by thefe Declarers.; fince the power hath been wholly in their Hands, and few or no forces pretending for the King in appearance againft them ; (His Armies being for
- moft

moſt part of the time disbanded, and His Townes and Garriſons reſigned.)

In a word, we ſhall preſent to the worlds review onely thoſe *Meſſages for Peace,* ſent from His Majeſty in theſe two laſt years, ſince a little before He laied down His *Sword,* and ceaſed from *Action* againſt them ; whereby it will be manifeſt enough, what little cauſe they have to ſpeak as they doe, in Commendation of themſelves and their owne good natures ; or to ſuggeſt of the King, as if He were ſo unperſwadable to this very day, that neither their owne *ſighs,* and *groans,* and *tears* will incline Him to be quiet, *nor the crying bloud of Fathers, Brothers, Children, and of many Hundred thouſand free-born Subjects in three great Kingdomes* can prevail with him to *deſiſt* from Cruelty and *deſtruction.* And then after this we ſhall deſire to ſee what *Evidence* themſelves can alleage for what they have ſaid ; we ſhall wiſh they would produce the *ſtrong reaſons* they have uſed, to ſhew thoſe *Humble addreſſes* which they have made, and doe ſo much boaſt of ; that they would let us Hear ſome of their *ſelf-denying ſtreins, affectionate expreſſions* or *devout Petitions,* which (as they infer) have ſo *reſpectfully* and *tenderly* flowed from them, ſo often, and ſo long, that thereby the *world* (to whom they appeal) may Judge in this caſe, betwixt their King and them : which if they are not able to doe, no queſtion but what they have voted of Him, will be generally concluded of them, *viz.* that they are worthy to be *interdicted all Humane ſociety,* to have no more *Meſſages* ſent, or *offers* made unto them : nor any *requeſts* or *Petitions* hereafter received from them ; And that the King ſhould ſay to them, as God doth to ſuch as they, *Becauſe I have called, and ye refuſed, I have ſtretched out my hand, and no man regarded, but have ſet at nought all my Councels,* and ſlighted all my motions, *therefore when your fear commeth as Deſolation, and your Deſtruction as a whirlewind, when diſtreſſe and anguiſh is upon you, then you ſhall call unto me, but I will not anſwer, you ſhall ſeek mercy from me, but you ſhall not find it ;* you ſhall *eat the fruit of your owne waies, and be filled with your owne deviſes :* As you have done, ſo ſhall it be done unto you.

His

His Majesties most Gracious Messages
for Peace, sent to the two Houses of Parliament at *Westminster* since the 5. of *Dec*.1645.

His Majesties first Message.

CHARLES R.

HIs Majesty being deeply sensible of the Continuation of this bloody and unnaturall Warre, cannot think Himself discharg'd of the duty He owes to God, or the affection and regard He hath to the preservation of His People, without the constant application of His earnest endeavours to finde some expedient for the speedy ending of these unhappy distractions, if that may be, doth therefore desire, That a Safe Conduct may be forthwith sent, for the Duke of *Richmond*, the Earle of *Southampton*, *John Ashburnham*, and *Jeffery Palmer* Esquires, and their Attendants, with Coaches, Horses, and other Accommodations for their Journey to *Westminster*, during their stay there, and return when they shall think fit. Whom His Majesty intends to send to the Lords & Commons assembled in the Parliament of *England* at *Westminster*, and the Commissioners of the Parliament of *Scotland*, furnished with such Propositions, as His Majesty is confident will be the Foundation of a happy and well-grounded Peace.

Given at the Court at Oxford *the* 5. *of* Decem.1645.

For the Speaker of the House of Peers pro tempore.

C   This

THis Message being received, a Letter was sent thereupon
from the *Speakers* of both *Houses* to Sir *Thomas Glemham*
(the then Governour of *Oxford*) promising an Answer to it *with
all convenient speed*, which His Majesty expected with silence accordingly *ten dayes*, and then solicites them again for the same
thing, which He had done before, as followeth.

His Majesties second Message.

CHARLES R.

HIs Majesty cannot but extremely wonder, that
after so many Expressions on your part, of a
deep and seeming sense of the miseries of this
afflicted Kingdome, and of the dangers incident to His
Person during the continuance of this unnaturall War,
your many great and so often repeated Protestations,
that the raising of these Arms hath been onely for the
necessary defence of Gods true Religion, His Majesties
Honour, Safety and Prosperity, the Peace, Comfort and
Security of His People, you should delay a Safe Conduct
to the persons mentioned in His Majesties Message of the
fifth of this instant *December*, which are to be sent unto
you with Propositions for a well-grounded Peace: A
thing so far from having been denyed at any time by His
Majesty, whensoever you have desired the same, that He
believes it hath been seldome (if ever) practiced among
the most avowed and professed enemies, much lesse
from Subjects to their King. But His Majesty is resolved, that no discouragements whatsoever shall make
Him faile of His part, in doing His uttermost endeavours to put an end to these Calamities, which if not in
time prevented, must prove the ruine of this unhappy
Na-

Nation; And therefore doth once again deſire, That a ſafe Conduct may be forthwith ſent for thoſe perſons expreſſed in His former Meſſage, and doth therefore Conjure you, as you will anſwer to Almighty God, in that day when he ſhal make inquiſition for all the Bloud that hath and may yet be ſpilt in this unnaturall War, as you tender the preſervation and eſtabliſhment of the true Religion; by all the Bonds of Duty and Allegiance to your King, or compaſſion to your bleeding, and unhappy Country, and of Charity to your ſelves, that you diſpoſe your hearts to a true ſenſe, and imploy all your faculties in a more ſerious endevour, together with His Majeſty, to ſet a ſpeedy end to theſe waſting Diviſions, and then He ſhall not doubt, but that God will yet again give the bleſſing of Peace to this diſtracted Kingdom.

Given at the Court at Oxford, *the* 15. *of December,* 1645.

For the Speaker of the Houſe
of Peers pro tempore.

THis Meſſage ſeconding the former, ſpake (as many others had done) His Majeſties earneſtneſſe for *Peace*; and how much affected He was with his peoples miſeries in the want of it: but 'tis thought meet (by them to whom 'tis ſent) *to make His Heart more ſicke, by delaying His hopes*; and therefore (neglecting their owne promiſe of returning an Anſwer *with all convenient ſpeed)* they cauſe him to wait *ten daies* longer, at the end of which time they ſeemed as far from remembring either *Him,* or *them-Jelves* as at the beginning: which His Majeſty obſerving, and withall conceiving this unwillingnes in them to admit of *Peace,* might be for that *He* had motioned to ſend it by others, apprehended becauſe they had (in pretence at leaſt) ſought ſo long to injoy His preſence, that if himſelf ſhould carry it, they would undoubtedly both imbrace *that,* and reverence *Him*; and thereupon offers to go unto them, and to Treat *perſonally* with them about the ſame:

C 2 yea

yea and to make the furer way to Himself with this great Blessing
(in the behalf of His people) He resolves to *buy* their consent, if he
cannot *beg* it, by receding so much from His owne *rights*, as none
of His Predecessours ever did : for supposing the point of their
owne *security*, to be the maine obstacle in the Businesse ; He offers
to part with the *Militia* it self out of His owne Hands for a season : and to this purpose, omitting all Expostulations for their so
High neglect, and contempt of Him, in not answering His former Messages ; He writes to them, as followeth :

His Majesties third Message.

CHARLS R.

NOtwithstanding the strange and unexpected delaies (which can be presidented by no former
times) to His Majesties two former Messages,
His Majesty will lay aside all Expostulations, as rather
serving to lose time, then to contribute any remedy to
the evils, which (for the present) do afflict this distracted
Kingdom; Therefore without farther Preamble, His Majesty thinks it most necessary to send these Propositions
this way, which He intended to do by the Persons mentioned in His former Messages, though He well knows
the great disadvantage, which Overtures of this kind
have, by the want of being accompanied by wel-instru-
cted Messengers.

His Majesty conceiving that the former Treaties have
hitherto proved ineffectuall, chiefly for want of power
in those persons that Treated, as likewise, because those
from whom their power was derived (not possibly having the particular informations of every severall debate) could not give so clear a Judgment as was requisite in so important a businesse ; If therefore His Majesty
                                                    may

may have the engagement of the two Houſes of Parliament at *Weſtminſter,* the Commiſſioners of the Parliament of *Scotland,* the Major, Aldermen, Common-
Councel, and Militia of *London,* of the chief Commanders in Sir *Thomas Fairfax's* Army, as alſo thoſe in the
Scots Army, for His Majeſties free and ſafe coming to,
& abode in *London* or *Weſtminſter,* with ſuch of His Servants now attending Him, and their Followers, not ex-
ceeding in all the number of 300.) for the ſpace of forty
daies, and after the ſaid time for his free and ſafe repair
to any of His Garriſons of *Oxford, Worceſter,* or *Newark,*
(which His Majeſty ſhall nominate at any time before
His going from *London* or *Weſtminſter*) His Majeſty
propounds to have a Perſonall Treaty with the two
Houſes of Parliament at *Weſtminſter,* and the Commiſſioners of the Parliament of *Scotland,* upon all matters
which may conduce to the reſtoring of Peace and happineſſe to theſe miſerably diſtracted Kingdoms; And to
begin with the three Heads which were Treated on at
Uxbridge. And for the better clearing of His Majeſties
earneſt and ſincere intentions of putting an end to theſe
unnaturall Diſtractions, (knowing that point of ſecurity may prove the greateſt obſtacle to this moſt bleſſed
work) His Majeſty therefore Declares, That He is willing to commit the great Truſt of the *Militia* of this
Kingdom, for ſuch time, and with ſuch Powers, as are
expreſt in the Paper delivered by His Majeſties Commiſſioners at *Uxbridge,* the 6. of *February* laſt, to theſe
Perſons following, *viz.* The Lord *Privy Seal,* the Duke
of *Richmond,* the Marqueſſe of *Hertford,* the Marqueſſe
of *Dorcheſter,* the Earl of *Dorſet,* Lord *Chamberlain,* the
Earl of *Northumberland,* the Earl of *Eſſex,* Earl of *South-
hampton,* Earl of *Pembroke,* Earl of *Salisbury,* Earl of

Mancheſter,

Manchester, Earl of *Warwick*, Earl of *Denbigh*, Earl of *Chichester*, Lord *Say*, Lord *Seymour*, Lord *Lucas*, Lord *Lexington*, Mr. *Denzill Hollis*, Mr. *Pierrepoint*, Mr. *Henry Bellasis*, Mr. *Richard Spencer*, Sir *Thomas Fairfax*, Master *John Ashburnham*, Sir *Gervas Clifton*, Sir *Henry Vane junior*, Mr. *Robert Wallop*, Mr. *Thomas Chichely*, Master *Oliver Cromwell*, and Mr. *Philip Skippon*, supposing that these are Persons against whom there can be no just exception: But if this doth not satisfie, then His Majesty offers to name the one half, and leave the other to the election of the two Houses of Parliament at *Westminster*, with the Powers and Limitations before mentioned.

Thus His Majesty calls God and the World to witnesse, of His sincere Intentions and reall Endevours, for the composing and setling of these miserable Distractions, which He doubts not, but by the blessing of God, will soon be put to a happy Conclusion, if this His Majesties offer be accepted; Otherwise He leaves all the World to Judge, who are the Continuers of this unnaturall War. And therefore He once more Conjures you, by all the Bonds of Duty you owe to God and your King, to have so great a Compassion on the bleeding and miserable Estate of your Country, That you joyne your most serious and hearty Endevours with His Majesty, to put a happy and speedy end to these present Miseries.

Given at the Court at Oxford *the 26 of December,* 1645.

For the Speaker of the House of Peers pro tempore,
To be Communicated to the two Houses of Parliament at Westminster, *and to the Commissioners of the Parliament of* Scotland.

While

WHile this Message was in the way of passage to them, this ensuing Paper (which seems to relate to the two former) comes from them, after 20 daies *serious Consideration*, (as themselves speak) for so long the *Lords and Commons of the Parliament of England*, together with the *Commissioners of the Parliament of Scotland*, were deep in consultation about the framing of it: it conteins only two things; a *Commendation* of themselves; and a *Deniall* of the Kings request, for a safe Conduct unto His *Commissioners* to Treat for *Peace:* 'tis this which follows:

May it please your *Majesty,*

THe *Lords and Commons Assembled in the Parliament of* England *at* Westminster, *have received your Letters of the fifth & fifteenth of this instant* December, *and having, together with the Commissioners of the Parliament of* Scotland, *taken the same into their serious consideration, do humbly return this Answer.*

They have in all their Actions manifested to Your Majesty *and the World, their sincere and earnest desires, that a safe and well grounded Peace might be setled in Your three Kingdoms, and for the obtaining so great a Blessing, shall ever pray to God, and use their utmost endevours, and beseech Your Majesty to believe; that their not sending a more speedy Answer, hath not proceeded from any intention to retard the means of putting an end to these present Calamities by a happy Peace, but hath been occasioned by the Considerations and Debates necessary in a businesse of so great importance, wherein both Kingdoms are so much concerned.*

As to Your Majesties desire of a safe Conduct for the coming hither of the Duke of Richmond, *the Earl of* Southampton, John Ashburnham *and* Jeffrey Palmer *Esquires, with Propositions to be the foundation of a happy and well grounded Peace, They finding that former Treaties have been made use of for other ends under the pretence of Peace, and have proved delatory, and unsuccessfull, cannot give way to a safe Conduct according to Your Majesties desire; But both Houses of the Parliament of* England, *having now under their Consideration Propositions and Bills for the setling of a safe and well grounded Peace, which are speedily to be communicated to the Commissioners*

missioners of the Kingdom of Scotland, *do resolve after mutuall a-greement of both Kingdoms to present them with all speed to Your Majesty.*

Westminster the
25. December, 1645.

Gray *of* Wark Speaker of the House of Peers *pro tempore.*
William Lenthall Speaker of the House of Commons.

WE have read of a proud *Pope,* that made His Lord the *Emperour* seeking for a *Treaty* with Him, wait three daies before he would grant it : but never till this Age was it heard or read, that *Humble and Loyall Subjects* (as these men call themselves) did force their Soveraigne to wait twenty daies for an Answer to a like request, and then return Him. a flat deniall : But His majesty had been too long, and too well acquainted with this *perverseneſſe* of theirs ; and being (in His meaſure) like Him whose *Vicegerent* He is, of great patience and long-ſuffering, paſſeth by again, this their unreverend Carriage and demeanour towards Him, without any expoſtulation about the ſame, being ever carefull, to ſhun and avoid what might in likelyhood hinder His pious deſigne, of obtaining *Peace* unto his people : and therefore preſſeth again His laſt motion in his third Meſſage for a *perſonall Treaty* in theſe words,

His *Majesties fourth Meſſage.*

CHARLS·R.

ALthough the Meſſage ſent by Sir *Peter Killegrew,* may juſtly require an expoſtulatory Anſwer, yet His Majeſty laies that aſide, as not ſo proper for His preſent Endevours ; leaving all the World to judge, whether His Propoſition for a Perſonall Treaty, or the flat deniall of a ſafe Conduct for Perſons to begin a Treaty, be greater ſignes of a reall Intention to Peace ; and

and shall now onely insist upon His former Message of the 26 of this *December*. That upon His repair to *Westminster*, He doubts not but so to joyne His Endeavours with His two Houses of Parliament, as to give just satisfaction, not onely concerning the businesse of *Ireland*, but also for the setling of a way for the payment of the Publike- Debts, as well to the *Scots*, and to the City of *London*, as others. And as already He hath shewn a fair way for the setling of the *Militia*, so He shall carefully Endeavour in all other Particulars, that none shall have cause to complain for want of security, whereby just Jealousies may arise to hinder the continuance of the desired Peace. And certainly this Proposition of a Personall Treaty could never have entred into His Majesties Thoughts, if He had not resolved to make apparent to all the World, that the Publike good and Peace of this Kingdom, is farre dearer to Him then the respect of any particular Interest. Wherefore none can oppose this Motion, without a manifest demonstration, that He particularly envies His Majesty should be the chief Author in so blessed a Work, besides the declaring Himself a direct opposer of the happy Peace of these Nations. To conclude, whosoever will not be ashamed, that His fair and specious Protestations should be brought to a true and Publike Test; and those who have a reall sence, and doe truely commiserate the miseries of their bleeding Countrey, let them speedily and cheerfully embrace His Majesties Proposition for His Personall Treaty at *Westminster*, which, by the blessing of God, will undoubtedly to these now distracted Kingdomes, restore the hap-

D

pinesse

pineſſe of a long wiſht for, and laſting Peace.
Given at the Court at Oxford, *the* 29 *day of* December, 1645.

For the Speaker of the Houſe of Peers pro tempore,
to be Communicated to the two Houſes of Parliament at Weſtminſter, *and the Commiſſioners of the Parliament of* Scotland.

THis Meſſage (as it ſeems) was very *unpleaſing*, and ſpake the King very *troubleſome*, in being ſo importunate for *Peace*, and to come amongſt them, whoſe *preſence* next to that of God, would be the greateſt torment to them: Wherefore to let him know, that Ambaſſadors for Peace are never welcome, but to thoſe that love it ; and to give him a gueſſe what Himſelf ſhould find if He came within their reach, they kept His *Meſſenger* as their Priſoner, and returned ſilence to His *Meſſage* : hereupon His Majeſty having waited their Leaſure full twenty daies longer (*viz.* from *Dec.* 26. to *Jan.* 15.) and hearing no news of either, ſends to inquire after His *Trumpet*, and withall moves again to the ſame purpoſe as before, inlarging His offers for what He deſires, and recedes further yet from His owne Rights, for His Peoples quiet, in theſe words :

His Majeſties fifth Meſſage.

CHARLS R.

BUt that theſe are times, wherein nothing is ſtrange, it were a thing much to be marvailed at, what ſhould cauſe this unparalell'd long detention of His Majeſties Trumpet, ſent with His Gracious Meſſage of the 26 of *December* laſt ; Peace being the only Subject of it, and His Majeſties Perſonall Treaty, the means propoſed for it. And it were almoſt as great a wonder, that

His

His Majeſty ſhould be ſo long from inquiring after it, if
that the hourly expectation thereof, had not, in ſome
meaſure ſatisfied His Impatience : But leſt His Majeſty
by His long ſilence, ſhould condemn Himſelf of Care-
leſneſſe in that, which ſo much concerns the good of all
His People, He thinks it high time to inquire after His
ſaid *Trumpeter*; For ſince all men who pretend any good-
neſs, muſt deſire Peace ; and that all men know Treaties
to be the beſt and moſt Chriſtian way to procure it, and
there being as little queſtion, that His Majeſties Perſonal
Preſence in it, is the likelieſt way to bring it to a happy
Iſſue ; He judges there muſt be ſome ſtrange variety of
accidents, which cauſeth this moſt tedious delay; wherefore His Majeſty earneſtly deſires to have a ſpeedy Account of His former Meſſage, the ſubject whereof is
Peace, and the means His Perſonall preſence at *Weſtmin-*
ſter, where the Government of the Church being ſetled,
as it was in the times of the happy and glorious Reigns
of Queen *Eliʒabeth* and King *James*, and full Liberty
for the eaſe of their Conſciences, who will not communicate in that Service eſtabliſhed by Law, and likewiſe
for the free and publike uſe of the *Directory* (preſcribed,
and by Command of the two Houſes of Parliament,
now practiſed in ſome parts of the City of *London*) to
ſuch as ſhall deſire to uſe the ſame, and all Forces being
agreed to be Disbanded, His Majeſty will then forthwith (as He hath in His Meſſage of the 29 of *December*
laſt, already offered) joyn with His two Houſes of Parliament, in ſetling ſome way for the payment of the
publike Debts to His *Scots* Subjects, the City of *Lon-*
don, and others : And His Majeſty having propoſed a
fair way, for the ſetling of the *Militia*, which now by
this long delay, ſeems not to be thought ſufficient ſecu-

rity :

rity: His Majesty (to shew how really He will imploy Himself at His coming to *Westminster*) for making this a lasting Peace, and taking away all jealousies, (how groundlesse soever) will endeavour upon debate with His two Houses, so to dispose of it (as likewise of the businesse of *Ireland*) as may give to them and both Kingdoms just satisfaction; not doubting also, but to give good contentment to His two Houses of Parliament in the choice of the Lord Admirall, the Officers of State and others, if His two Houses, by their ready inclinations to Peace shall give Him encouragement thereunto. Thus His Majesty having taken occasion by His just impatience so to explain His intentions, that no man can doubt of a happy Issue to this succeeding Treaty: If now, there shall be so much as a delay of the same, He calls God and the World to witnesse, who they are, that not only hinder, but reject this Kingdoms future happinesse, It being so much the stranger, that His Majesties coming to *Westminster*, (which was first the greatest pretence for taking up Arms)should be so much as delayed, much lesse not accepted or refused; But His Majesty hopes, that God will no longer suffer the malice of Wicked men to hinder the Peace of this too much afflicted Kingdom.

Given at the Court at Oxford, *the* 15 *of* January, 1645.

For the Speaker of the House of Peers pro tempore, *To be Communicated to the two Houses of Parliament at* Westminster, *and the Commissioners of the Parliament of* Scotland.

CAn Subjects desire more, or to have their King offer more, then is here tendred? sure no good Christian Subjects can desire so much, or be content to have their King recede so far from
Himself

Himself for their fakes : But by this, and the preceding *Messages*, we see what the King hath bidden for the purchase of *Peace*, and a Treaty with them ; now we shall have a glimpse of what they thought fit to aske of Him for their *leave* to let Him come, and speak with them, after they had fasted, prayed, and fought five years to fetch Him to His Parliament : for immediately after His sending this last most gracious Message, there came to His Majesties hands as the effect of His Four former, and the reward of His forty daies waiting this insuing Paper, which contains only a parcell of such scandalous and crosse speeches, as shamelesse women are wont to cast up against those they raile upon, and mean to live in Contention with, which notwithstanding the world (supposed to be as void of Reason, as themselves are of Religion) must interpret an *Humble Addresse unto His Majesty for Peace*, because it begins with *May it please your Majesty, We your Humble and Loyall Subjects*, for 'tis one of those *Addresses*, which (in the beginning of their late Declaration) they say *the world well knows to have been so fruitlesse*, wherein they have *yeilded up their wills, Affections, Reason, Judgment, and all for obtaining a true peace or good Accommodation*, it follows in these very words,

May it please your Majesty,

WE *Your Humble and Loyall Subjects of both Kingdoms, have received Your Letters of the 26 and 29 of* December *last; unto which we humbly return this Answer.*

That there hath been no delay on our parts, but what was necessary in a businesse of so great consequence, as is expressed in our former Letter to Your Majesty.

Concerning the personall Treaty desired by Your Majesty, There having been so much innocent bloud of Your good Subjects shed in this War, by Your Majesties Commands and Commissions, Irish Rebels brought over into both Kingdoms, and endeavours to bring over more into both of them, as also Forces from Forraign parts ; Your Majesty being in Arms in these parts, the Prince in the head of an Army in the West, divers Towns made Garrisons, and kept in Hostility by Your Majesty against the Parliament of England *: There being also Forces in* Scotland *against that Parliament and Kingdom by Your Majesties Commission : The War in* Ireland *fomented and prolonged*

by

by Your Majesty, whereby the three Kingdoms are brought neer to utter ruine and destruction. We conceive, That untill satisfaction and security be first given to both your Kingdoms, Your Majesties coming hither cannot be convenient, nor by us assented unto. Neither can we apprehend it a means conducing to Peace, That Your Majesty should come to Your Parliament for a few daies, with any thoughts of leaving it ; especially with intentions of returning to Hostility against it. And We do observe, That Your Majesty desires the Ingagement, not only of the Parliaments, but of the Lord Mayor, Aldermen, Common-Councell, and Militia of the City of London, *the chief Commanders of Sir* Thomas Fairfax's *Army, and those of the* Scots *Army, which is against the Priviledges and Honour of the Parliaments, those being joyned with them, who are subject and subordinate to their Authority.*

That which Your Majesty against the freedom of the Parliaments inforces in both Your Letters with many earnest expressions, as if in no other way then that propounded by Your Majesty, the Peace of Your Kingdoms could be established, Your Majesty may please to remember, that in Our last Letter, We did Declare, That Propositions from both Kingdoms were speedily to be sent to Your Majesty, which We conceive to be the only way for attaining a happy and well-grounded Peace, and Your Majesties assent unto those Propositions, will be an effectuall meanes for giving satisfaction and security to Your Kingdoms : will assure a firm Union between the two Kingdoms, as much desired by each other as for themselves ; And settle Religion and secure the Peace of the Kingdom of Scotland, *whereof neither is so much as mentioned in Your Majesties Letters.*

And in proceeding according to these just and necessary grounds for the putting an end to the bleeding Calamities of these Nations, Your Majesty may have the Glory to be a Principall Instrument in so happy a Work ; and We (however mis-interpreted) shall approve our selves to God and the World, to be reall and sincere in seeking a safe and wel-grounded Peace. Westminster, 13. Jan. 1645.

Grey of Wark, Speaker of the House of Peers *pro tempore.*
William Lenthall, Speaker of the House of Commons.

For Your Majesty.

Signed in the name and by warrant of the Commissioners of the Parliament of Scotland.
BALMERINOTH.

THeir *silence* was bad, and shewed great insolency, but their *Language* is far worse, and speaks much more, for their stile and matter in this Paper declares them to be *men most unreasonable*, even such as the Apostle praies God *to be delivered from*, and shews clearly on which side the obstruction to *peace* lies : we see herein upon what Conditions the King might have been admitted (after so many Messages) into the presence of His *Humble and Loyall Subjects* : if He would but have owned the guilt of that innocent bloud *themselves had shed*, bin content to be dawbed with *their crimes*, laid down His *Armes*, given up His *Garrisons*, call'd in His *Commissions*, deserted His *Friends*, and deliver'd up *Himself* absolutely without any security into their Hands, with such a submission as they should prescribe, which should have been no other, then might have spoke His approbation of all they have said or done against Himself and this Kingdome to be just and right ; then His *Humble and Loyall Subjects* would have vouchsafed to cast a look upon Him, and deign'd so far as to have spoke a word with him.

Herein also besides the Conditions of a *Treaty* are discovered divers *faults* in His Majesties late Messages, which neither Himself nor any other was able to have discern'd, but the two Parliaments of *England* and *Scotland* after a diligent search, having sat close some weeks about it, (for they were not idle all the 40 daies of the Kings waiting) did in their deep wisdomes descry and find them out, and then thought fit (that their Soveraigne might not sleep in His sins) to admonish His Majesty of them : as , : i : / !

1. His requiring of them *ingagement for His own security* if He came amongst them, which was a great errour and mistake in Him, for though He be a *David*, and a man after Gods owne heart, yet they are not *subjects* of the same stamp as *Davids* were, who thought their King worth *ten thousand of themselves*.

2. This request of His, was (in their judgements) against the *Priviledge and Honour of Parliament*, for the speciall Priviledge of this Parliament, or rather the swaying faction in the same, is to *destroy* if they can, and not to *preserve* the King at all.

3. His mentioning the *Mayor, Aldermen, Common-Councell, and Militia* of the City, (as if He believed Himself to have any
interest

interest in them, and that they were concern'd to ingage for His security) they give Him to understand, was another grand *mistake* in Him ; for all they, together with Sir *Thomas Fairfax* his Army, and the *Scots* too, are *their* subjects and not *His*, and subordinate to *their* Authority, and therefore for *Him* to expect any *ingagement* for safety from any of *them*, was directly also (in their sense) against the *Honour and Priviledge of Parliament*.

Nay 4. they give His Majesty to know, that He had not onely sinned thus, against the *Honour and Priviledge of Parliament*, but also against the very *freedome* of it, by His propounding with so many *earnest expressions* a Personall Treaty, as the *way to a Peace* ; which they interpret no other then a plaine *enforcement* upon the *Liberty* of Parliament, or a violent *rape* upon their wisdome ; as if *they* had not Brains enow, to find out some other *way*, then that was which His Majesty had propounded : But truly (with their favour) this Errour might more prudently have been passed by, and the aggravation of it omitted ; had they but remembred how often themselves had told the world, that all their fighting was but *to bring the King home from His evill Counsellours, to Treat in Person with His Parliament* : for what may the world now think of these wise men ? may they not liken them to *little Children*, who in a crosse peevish humour, wil none of *that thing* when offered to them, but throw it away, which before they had cried and roared for ? the old and true way to a *Peace* between different parties, hath alwaies been by *Treaty*, and so was it hitherto judged by these men, (as themselves told us) but now they dislike it, only because the King propounds it : And another way, they have devised, and that must be by *Propositions* of their owne making ; which by this their *Preface* are promised to be such as *Benhadad* sent to the King of *Israel*, neither good for Him, nor for His people, but destructive unto both.

But His *sacred Majesty*, the true *mirror* of wisdome, meeknesse, and patience, receiving from them (after divers *Messages* and forty daies waiting) only this reproachfull Paper, (which was able to stir passion in a very *Moses*) doth send back on the very same day, without returning one word of ill Language, this ensuing Answer :

His

His *Majesties sixt Message.*

CHARLES R.

HIs Majesty thinks not fit now to answer those
asperfions which are returned as arguments for
His not admittance to *Westminster* for a Perfonall Treaty, because it would inforce a ftyle not futable
to His end, it being the Peace of thefe miferable Kingdoms : yet thus much He cannot but fay to thofe who
have fent Him this Anfwer, That if they had confidered
what they have done themfelves in occafioning the fhed-
ding of fo much innocent bloud, by withdrawing themfelves from their duty to Him, in a time when He had
granted fo much to His Subjects, and in violating the
knowne Laws of the Kingdome to draw an exorbitant
power to themfelves over their fellow Subjects, (to fay
no more to do as they have done) they could not have
given fuch a falfe character of His Majefties actions.
Wherefore His Majefty muft now remember them, that
having fome howers before His receiving of their laft
Paper of the 13. of *Jan.* fent another Meffage to them of
the 15. wherein by divers particulars He inlargeth Himfelf to fhew the reality of His endevours for Peace by His
defired perfonall Treaty (which He ftill conceives to be
the likelieft way to attain to that bleffed end) He thinks
fit by this Meffage to call for an Anfwer to that, and indeed to all the former. For certainly no rationall man
can think their laft Paper can be any Anfwer to His former demands, the fcope of it being, that becaufe there
is a War, therefore there fhould be no Treaty for Peace.
And is it poffible to expect that the Propofitions men-

tioned

tioned ſhould be the grounds of a Laſting Peace, when the Perſons that ſend them will not endure to hear their own King ſpeak ? But whatever the ſucceſſe hath been of His Majeſties former Meſſages, or how ſmall ſoever His hopes are of a better, conſidering the high ſtrain of thoſe who deal with His Majeſty, yet He will neither want fatherly bowels to His Subjects in generall, nor will He forget that God hath appointed Him for their King with whom He Treats. Wherefore He now demands a ſpeedy Anſwer to His laſt and former Meſſages.

Given at our Court at Oxon *this* 17. *of* Jan. 1645.

For the Speaker of the Houſe of Peers pro tempore, *to be communicated,* &c.

THeſe earneſt deſires of His Majeſty for a *ſpeedy* Anſwer ſhall nothing prevail with them to *haſten* the ſame, for His unparallel'd meekneſſe in paſſing by ſuch unheard-of *Affronts*, without return of any paſſionate expreſſion, is ſo high a vexation to their black and ungodly ſouls; that they reſolve in themſelves to make Him wait above three times forty daies longer now, before He ſhall get a word more from them, let Him ſend as oft as He will to ſolicite for it : which purpoſed contempt though His Majeſty in His *Candour* and *Charity* did not (haply) at that preſent fancy of them ; yet being too well acquainted with their diſpoſitions, He conceived they might make ſome ill uſe among His People, of His ſilence to their impediments objected againſt the *Perſonall Treaty* propounded by Him ; and therefore thought meet ſeven daies after to ſpeak ſomewhat in Confutation of thoſe their frivolous Arguments, and again to urge the thing ; as the only likely way of ſetling *Peace* unto His People ; who from hence may obſerve, that no rudeneſſe or inſolency towards Him, nor unjuſt aſperſions of Him, are able to divert Him from purſuing the means of their welfare : His words are theſe,

His

His Majesties seventh Message.

CHARLS R.

THe procuring Peace to thefe Kingdoms by Treaty, is fo much defired by His Majefty, that no un-
juft afperfions whatfoever, or any other difcou-
ragements fhall make Him defift from doing His endevour therein, untill He fhall fee it altogether impoffible: and therefore hath thought fitting fo far only to
make reply to that Paper or Anfwer which He hath received of the 13 of this inftant *Jan.* as may take away
thofe ObjeStions which are made againft His-Majefties
coming to *Weftminfter,* expeSting ftill an Anfwer to His
Meffages of the 15, and 17. which He hopes by this time
have begotten better thoughts and refolutions, in the
Members of both *Houfes.* And firft therefore, Whereas
in the faid laft Paper it is objeSted as an impediment to
His Majefties perfonal Treaty, that much innocent bloud
hath been fhed in this War, by His Majefties Commiffions, &c. He will not now difpute (it being apparent to
all the World by whom this bloud hath been fpilt) but
rather preffeth that there fhould be no more: and (to
that end only) He hath defired this perfonall Treaty, as
judging it the moft immediate means to abolifh fo many
horrid confufions in all His Kingdoms. And it is no argument, to fay, That there fhall be no fuch perfonall
Treaty, becaufe there have been Wars, it being a ftrong
inducement to have fuch a Treaty to put an end to the
War. Secondly, that there fhould be no fuch perfonall
Treaty, becaufe fome of His *Irifh* SubjeSts have repaired
to His affiftance in it, feems an argument altogether as

E 2   ftrange

strange as the other ; as alwaies urging that there should
be no Physick, becaufe the party is fick : And in this
particular it hath been often obferved unto them, that
thofe, whom they call *Irish*, who have fo expreffed their
Loyalty to their Soveraigne, were indeed (for the moft
part) fuch English Proteftants, as had been formerly
fent into *Ireland* by the two Houfes, impoffibilitated to
ftay there any longer by the neglect of thofe that fent
them thither, who fhould there have better provided for
them. And for any Forrain forces, it is too apparent
that *their* Armies have fwarmed with them, when His
Majefty hath had very few or none. And whereas, for a
third impediment, it is alleaged that the Prince is in the
head of an Army in the *Weft*, and that there are divers
Garrifons ftil kept in his Majefties *obedience*,& that there
are Forces in *Scotland* ; it muft be as much confeffed, as
that as yet there is no peace ; and therefore it is defired,
that by fuch a perfonall Treaty, all thefe impediments
may be removed. And it is not here amiffe to put them
in mind, how long fince His Majefty did preffe a disbanding of all Forces on both fides ; the refufing whereof,
hath been the caufe of this objection. And whereas exception is taken, that there is a time limited in the Pro-
pofition for His Majefties perfonall Treaty, thereupon
inferring, that He fhould again return to Hoftility, His
Majefty protefteth that He feeks this Treaty to avoid future Hoftility, and to procure a lafting peace, and if He
can meet with like inclinations to Peace in thofe He defires to Treat with, He will bring fuch affections and refolutions in Himfelf, as fhal end all thefe unhappy bloudy differences. As for thofe ingagements which His Majefty hath defired for His fecurity, whofoever fhall call
to mind the particular occafions that enforced His Majefty

jefty to leave His City of *London* and *Westminster,* will judge His demand very reasonable and necessary for His safety. But He no way conceiveth how the L. Major, Aldermen, Common-Councell, and Militia of *London,* were either subject or subordinate to that Authority which is alleaged, as knowing neither Law nor practice for it : and if the two Armies be, He believes it is more then can be parallel'd by any former times in this Kingdom. Nor can His Majesty understand how His Majesties seeking of a Personall Security can be any breach of Priviledge : it being likely to be infringed by hindering His Majesty from coming freely to His two Houses. As for the Objection that His Majesty omitted to mention the setling Religion, and securing the Peace of His Native Kingdom, His Majesty declares, that He conceives that it was included in His former, and hath been particularly mentioned in his latter Message of the 15 present. But, for their better satisfaction, he again expresseth that it was, and ever shal be, both his meaning and endevour in this Treaty desired ; and it seems to him very clear, that there is no way for a finall ending of such distractions as afflict this Kingdom, but either by Treaty or Conquest, the latter of which his Majesty hopes none will have the impudency or impiety to wish for : and for the former, if his Personall assistance in it be not the most likely way, let any reasonable man judge : when by that means not only all unnecessary delaies will be removed, but even the greatest difficulties made easie. And therefore he doth now again earnestly insist upon that proposition, expecting to have a better answer upon mature consideration. And can it be imagined that any Propositions will be so effectuall, being formed before a personall Treaty, as such as are framed and propounded up-

on

on a full debate on both fides? Wherefore his Majefty, who is moft concerned in the good of his People, and is moft defirous to reftore peace and happineffe to his three Kingdoms, doth again inftantly defire an Anfwer to his faid former Meffages, to which he hath hitherto recei-ved none.

Given at our Court at Oxon *the* 24. *of* Jan. 1645.

To the Speaker of the Houfe of Peers pro tempore, *to be communicated to the two Houfes of Parlia-ment at* Weftminfter, *and to the Commiſſioners of the Parliament of* Scotland.

FEw that ventured their lives to fetch home the King (at the inftigation of thefe men)or that heard their Preachers pray fo oft ,*that God would incline His Majefties heart to come unto His Par-liament,* would ever have believed, that He fhould thus be put to plead for His own admittance amongft them, (who pretended to be fo fond of His Company;) or to Anfwer fuch *cavils* againft the fame, as He hath here done, if they had not feen them objected under their own Hands:nor would any have been perfwaded(had there not been fomewhat extant to evidence the fame) that thefe men could (after all this) have affirmed, that themfelves *had yeil-ded up not only their wills and Affections, but alfo their reafon and judgment for obtaining a good Accommodation with the King :* but now 'tis manifeft who they are that have abufed, gulled, and de-ceived the world ; and who have been the only *obftructers* unto *Peace,* and moft perfect *Enemies* thereunto : And yet 'tis no mervaile, that the wickedneffe of thefe notorious men was too deep and high for vulgar reaches, feeing His Majefty Himfelf af-ter all His experience, (being ftill ftraitned in fpirit by His owne Charity and goodneffe) was not yet able to fadome the fame, at His fending this feventh Meffage ; as may appear by His faying therein, that *He Hopes none will have that impudency and impiety, as to wifh an end to the diſtractions of this Kingdom, rather by Con-queſt then by Treaty :* for in very deed (as all the world are now perfwaded perſwaded ſince the publiſhing of their late Declaration) theſe men have had that *impudency* and *impiety* in them, even from the beginning, not onely to wiſh, but alſo to endevour the ſame ; therefore in vain did His Majeſty (as he ſince hath found) by this again, ſo inſtantly deſire an Anſwer to His former Meſſages for a *perſonal* meeting:And yet hoping(at leaſt)that importunity might prevail with theſe *unrighteous Judges*, (though intreaties will not) as it once did with one, *that feared neither God nor Man*, He re-ſolves to follow them ſtill with the ſame motion, which five daies after He doth, and that upon this occaſion.

His Majeſty was informed of the *Earl of* Glamorgans *unwar-ranted Agitation in Ireland*, and knowing that the manner of His *Humble and Loyal Subjects* at *Weſtminſter*,was to Honour Him,by heaping on Him the burden of others faults; He thinks it pious & meet to endevour to keep them from that ſin, by giving them a ſpeedy notice of the ſaid *Earls* doings, & of his own abſolute diſ-like of the ſame, which He evidences by His full approbation of that courſe which by Marqueſſe *Ormond*,and L.*Digby* was taken a-gainſt him, Proteſting ſolemnly that *he* never had knowledge of any ſuch *capitulation* or *Treaty* til He *heard of the Earls Arreſt and reſtraint* for making the ſame; diſavowing the Articles by Him, concluded and ſigned, as *deſtructive both to Church and State, re-pugnant to His Majeſties publick profeſſions and known reſolutions*, and ſo *hazardous to the blemiſhing His Reputation* ; and giving Commandement to the *Lord Lieutenant* and *Councell* of that Kingdom,to proceed againſt the ſaid *Earl*, for this His grand of-fence, committed out of *falſneſſe, preſumption*, or *folly.*

And after this, His Majeſty falls again to His old work of im-portuning a *Treaty for Peace*, which He urgeth upon them, with renewed promiſes, larger conceſſions, greater ingagements of Himſelf, and further Explanations of His ſincere intentions to *truſt* them, to *pardon* them, to *ſecure* them, let the world read this which follows, and then judge, if any Heart that intends to acknowledge a King, can deſire more.

His

His *Majesties eighth Message.*

CHARLS R.

His Majesty having received Information from the Lord Lieutenant and Councell in *Ireland* ; That the Earl of *Glamorgan* hath, without His, or their directions or privity, entred into a Treaty with some Commissioners on the Roman Catholique Party there, and also drawn up and agreed unto certain Articles with the said Commissioners, highly derogatory to his Majesties honour and Royall Dignity, and most prejudiciall unto the Protestant Religion and Church there in *Ireland* : Whereupon the said Earl of *Glamorgan* is arrested, upon suspition of High Treason, and imprisoned by the said Lord Lieutenant and Councell, at the instance and by the Impeachment of the L. *Digby*, who (by reason of his Place and former Imployment in these Affairs) doth best know how contrary that Proceeding of the said Earl hath been to his Majesties Intentions and Directions, and what great prejudice it might bring to his Affairs, if those Proceedings of the Earl of *Glamorgan*, should be any waies underftood to have been done by the directions, liking or approbation of his Majesty.

His Majesty, having in his former Messages for a Personall Treaty offered to give contentment to his two Houses in the Businesse of *Ireland* ; hath now thought fitting, the better to shew his clear Intentions, and to give satisfaction to his said Houses of Parliament, and the rest of his Subjects in all his Kingdoms ; to send

this

this Declaration to his said Houses containing the whole truth of the businesse, which is

That the Earle of *Glamorgan* having made offer unto Him to raise Forces in the Kingdom of *Ireland*, and to Conduct them into *England* for His Majesties Service, had a Commission to that purpose, and to that purpose only.

That he had no Commission at all to Treat of any thing else, without the privity and directions of the *Lord Lieutenant*, much lesse to Capitulate any thing concerning Religion, or any Propriety, belonging either to Church or Laity.

That it clearly appears by the *Lord Lieutenants* Proceedings with the said Earle, That he had no notice at all of what the said Earle had Treated and pretended to have capitulated with the *Irish*, untill by accident it came to his knowledge.

And His Majesty doth Protest, That untill such time as He had advertisement, that the Person of the said Earle of *Glamorgan* was Arrested and restrained, as is abovesaid, He never heard, nor had any kind of notice, that the said Earl had entred into any kind of Treaty or Capitulation with those *Irish* Commissioners: much lesse, that He had concluded or Signed those Articles so destructive both to Church and State, and so repugnant to His Majesties publique Professions, and known Resolutions.

And for the further vindication of His Majesties Honour and Integrity herein, He doth Declare, That He is so far from considering any thing contained in those Papers or Writings framed by the said Earl, and those Commissioners with whom he Treated, as He doth absolutely disavow him therein, and hath given Commandement

F

dement to the *Lord Lieutenant,* and the *Councell* there, to proceed againſt the ſaid Earl, as one, who, either out of falſeneſſe, preſumption, or folly, hath ſo hazarded the blemiſhing of His Majeſties Reputation with His good Subjeſts, and ſo impertinently framed thoſe Articles of his own head, without the Conſent, Privity, or Directions of His Majeſty, or the Lord Lieutenant, or any of His Majeſties Councell there. But true it is, That for the neceſſary preſervation of His Majeſties Proteſtant Subjeſts in *Ireland,* whoſe Caſe was daily repreſented unto Him to be ſo deſperate, His Majeſty had given Commiſſion to the Lord Lieutenant to Treat and Conclude ſuch a Peace there, as might be for the ſafety of that Crown, the preſervation of the Proteſtant Religion, and no way derogatory to His own Honour and publike Profeſſions.

But to the end, that His Majeſties reall intentions in this buſineſſe of *Ireland,* may be the more clearly underſtood, and to give more ample ſatisfaſtion to both Houſes of Parliament, and the Commiſſioners of the Parliament of *Scotland,* eſpecially concerning His Majeſties not being engaged in any Peace or Agreement there ; He doth deſire, if the two Houſes ſhall reſolve to admit of His Majeſties repair to *London,* for a Perſonall Treaty, (as was formerly propoſed) that ſpeedy notice be given thereof to His Majeſty, and a paſſe or ſafe Conduſt, with a blank ſent for a Meſſenger to be immediatly diſpatch'd into *Ireland,* to prevent any accident that may happen to hinder His Majeſties Reſolution of leaving the manageing of the buſineſſe of *Ireland* wholly to the two Houſes, and to make no Peace, there but with their conſent, which in caſe it ſhall pleaſe God to bleſſe His endevours in the Treaty with ſucceſſe, His Majeſty doth hereby engage Himſelf to do.   **And**

And for a further explanation of His Majeſties Intentions in His former Meſſages, He doth now Declare,
That if His Perſonall repair to *London* as aforeſaid, ſhall
be admitted, and a Peace thereon ſhall enſue, He will
then leave the nomination of the Perſons to be intruſted
with the *Militia,* wholly to His two Houſes, with ſuch
power and limitations as are expreſſed in the Paper delivered by His Majeſties Commiſſioners at *Uxbridge* the
6. of *Febr.* 1644. for the terme of Seven years, as hath
been deſired, to begin immediately after the concluſion
of the Peace, the disbanding of all Forces on both ſides,
and the diſmantling of the Garriſons erected ſince theſe
preſent Troubles, ſo as at the expiration of the time before mentioned, the power of the *Militia* ſhall entirely
revert and remain as before.

And for their further ſecurity, His Majeſty (the Peace
ſucceeding) will be content, that *pro hâc vice* the two
Houſes ſhall nominate the Admirall, Officers of State
and Judges, to hold their places during life, or *quâm diu
ſe bene geſſerint,* which ſhall be beſt liked, to be accomp-
table to none but the King, and the two Houſes of Parliament.

As for matter of Religion ; His Majeſty doth further
Declare, That by the liberty offered in his Meſſage of
the 15. preſent, for the eaſe of their Conſciences who
will not communicate in the Service already eſtabliſhed
by Act of Parliament in this Kingdom ; He intends that
all other Proteſtants behaving themſelves peaceably in
and towards the Civill Government, ſhall have the free
exerciſe of their Religion, according to their own way.

And for the totall removing of all Fears and Jealou-
ſies, His Majeſty is willing to agree, That upon the concluſion of Peace, there ſhall be a generall Act of Obli-

F 2

vion

vion and Free Pardon paſt by Acts of Parliaments in both his Kingdoms reſpectively.

And leſt it ſhould be imagined that in the making theſe Propoſitions, his Majeſties Kingdom of *Scotland*, and his Subjects there have been forgotten or neglected, his Majeſty Declares, That what is here mentioned touching the *Militia*, and the naming of Officers of State and Judges, ſhall likewiſe extend to his Kingdom of *Scotland*.

And now his Majeſty having ſo fully and clearly expreſſed his Intentions and deſires of making a happy and wel-grounded Peace, if any perſon ſhall decline that happineſſe by oppoſing of ſo apparent a way of attaining it, he will ſufficiently demonſtrate to all the world his intention and Deſigne can be no other, then the totall ſubverſion and change of the ancient and happy Government of this Kingdom under which the Engliſh Nation hath ſo long flouriſhed.

Given at the Court at Oxford *the 29 of* Jan. 1645.

For the Speaker of the Houſe of Peers pro tempore,
To be Communicated to the two Houſes of Parliament at Weſtminſter, *and the Commiſſioners of the Parliament of* Scotland.

HIs Majeſties *care* and *pains* in the former part of this Meſſage was wholly *ineffectuall* to the ends intended; for as if they had ſecretly vowed (as perhaps they have) to go contrary to *Him*, and *Christian Religion* in every thing, they took advantage from *this* very *buſineſſe of Ireland*, (thus diſclaimed by the King) to ſclaunder Him further and defame Him: to which purpoſe they publiſhed ſoon after certain Papers with this Title, *The Earl of* Glamorgans *negotiations, and colourable Comitment in Ireland*, that thereby it might be apprehended the King (like themſelves)

selves) had diſſembled, in all He had ſaid or writ about that matter. And in their *late Declaration* they moſt impudently affirm,
that His Majeſty gave a *private Commiſſion to the ſaid Earl*, com-
manding him, to manage it *with all poſſible ſecreſie*, and it contained (ſay they) ſuch *odious* and *ſhamefull things, as Himſelf bluſh'd
to owne*, or to *impart to His own Lieutenant, the Earl of* Ormond :
this they write upon their own teſtimony, as if they had been eye
and ear witneſſes of the ſame, and all the world were bound to
believe them : *ſed Deus vindex*, God ſhall judge and revenge too
upon them, the cauſe of *His Anointed*, to whom His Goſpel commands *Honour*, and themſelves have often ſworn *Reverence.*

And as His Majs.care in the former was *ineffectual*,ſo His *grace* in
the latter part of this Meſſage was altogether *fruitleſſe;*for though
Subjects (if Subjects) were they never ſo guilty, could wiſh for no
more then is there offered ; for there is *Liberty* for their Conſciences, *Safety* for their Perſons, *Security* for their Eſtates, *Greatneſſe* for their Deſires, and *Peace* to increaſe all, and all this but
for leave to let the reſt of His people (their fellow-Subjects, as
good men as themſelves,and much better,) live in peace by them ;
yet all will not do, nothing will work upon them, for (like Pope
Boniface the 8. of that name) they *came in like Foxes,* and therefore mean to *live like Lions,* though they *die like Dogs,* ſo that
Rebellion we ſee is a *ſin unpardonable* (like that againſt the *Holy
Ghoſt*) not becauſe it *cannot*, but becauſe it *will not* be forgiven.

His Majeſty after the ſending this laſt *Meſſage* of the 29. of *January* tarryes a moneth longer even till *Feb.* 28. in expectation of
ſomewhat from them in Anſwer to His longing deſires, and then
though He was apprehenſive how He had (by His often ſending)
hazarded His *Honour* to be queſtioned, as well as His proper *intereſts* to be divided or divorced from Him, yet to declare further ſtill to all the world,that His Peoples *Preſervation* was more
dear to Him then both, He doth once again in their behalf im-
portune theſe men for the Bleſſing of *Peace*, in theſe words,

His Majesties ninth Message.

CHARLES R.

His Majesty needs to make no excuse, though He sent no more Messages unto you: for He very well knows He ought not to doe it, if He either stood upon punctilio's of Honour, or His own private interest; the one being already call'd in question by His often sending; and the other assuredly prejudg'd if a Peace be concluded from that He hath already offered, He having therein departed with many of His undoubted Rights. But nothing being equally dear unto him, to the preservation of his people, his Majesty passeth by many scruples, neglects and delaies, and once more desires you to give him a speedy Answer to his last Message; for his Majesty believes it doth very well become him (after this very long delay) at last to utter his impatience, since that the goods and bloud of his Subjects cries so much for Peace.

Given at the Court at Oxford, *the 26 of* Febr. 1645.

For the Speaker of the House of Peers pro tempore,
To be Communicated to the two Houses of Parlia-
ment at Westminster, *and the Commissioners of*
the Parliament of Scotland.

As Christs *meeknes* and *mighty works* made his Enemies more *obdurate*, so the Kings *mildnes* and many *Messages* made these men more *obstinate*, who are as dumb to this last, as to the former: And though His Majesty tells them that *the Goods and bloud of His Subjects doth cry so much for Peace, that He shall be forced thereby to utter His impatience,* yet these hard-hearted men had rather hear those sad and lamentable *cries,* then listen to these *yearnings*

yearnings of their fathers Bowells ; nay, and they must be call'd and accounted *Patriots of their Country* for all this, and He, who is thus tenderly affected towards it, (in this its bleeding Condition) must be reckoned and reported the *Common Enemy* unto it : for they are not ashamed (notwithstanding these His many pantings and breathings after the Health of it) to appropriate unto Him their own Tigerly dispositions, and to tell the whole world in the first page of their late impudent *Declaration,* that neither the *sighs, Groans, tears, nor crying bloud, an heavy cry (say they) of Fa-thers, Brothers, Children, and of many hundred thousand free-born Subjects at once,* can perswade Him to pity or Compassion : Sure-ly could Satan help them to devise worse evill then is in them-selves, or then they have acted to cast upon the King, these His *Humble and Loyal Subjects* would not be so void of shame as thus to charge Him with their owne doings and Conditions.

Well, His Majesty after He had sent this last Message, waits yet another moneth for some Answer, though to as little purpose as before, He did but pursue the shaddow that fled from Him, by seeking *peace* at their hands, for they were resolved by *slighting* Him, to make him desist at length from *writing* thus to them. But behold the true Image of our most *patient God,* in this our most *Christian King,* who having to do with a like stif-necked and re-bellious people, as he of old had, thinks it His duty to follow him still in the same path, though with as little comfort or hopes of prevailing ; and hereupon sends the *tenth* time, and offers to come, and trust *Himself* wholly with them, if He might but have their own faith and promise for the *safety of His Person, Honour and Estate,* which themselves had so solemnly protested to defend; and that His friends (who had done according to their Duty and *Pro-testation*) might not (for the same) be deprived of their *Liberties* or *estates,* but injoy *both,* with a *freedome of Conscience* from un-lawfull Oaths : upon these sole Conditions He will pardon and forget all that was past on their sides, giving them what security themselves can devise, He will follow their advise (for the good of His People) rather then other mens ; and in a word, He will grant them as much, as till then they had ever *desired,* or made pretence unto, and all to procure a speedy Peace to these Afflicted Kingdoms. His words are these,

                                                                   His

His Majesties tenth Message.

CHARLS R.

NOtwithstandig the unexpected silence in stead of Answer to his Majesties many and gracious Messages to both Houses, whereby it may appear, that they desire to obtain their ends by Force, rather then Treaty, which may justly discourage his Majesty from any more overtures of that kind, yet his Majesty conceives He shall be much wanting to His duty to God, and in what He oweth to the safety of His people if He should not intend to prevent the great inconveniences that may otherwise hinder a safe and wel-grounded peace. His Majesty therefore now proposeth, that, so He may have the faith of both Houses of Parliament for the preservation of His Honour, Person, and Estate; and that Liberty be given to all those who do and have adhered to His Majesty to go to their own Houses, and there to live peaceably enjoying their Estates, all Sequestrations being taken off, without being compelled to take any Oath not enjoyned by the undoubted Laws of the Kingdom, or being put to any other molestation whatsoever, He will immediately disband all His Forces, and dismantle all His Garrisons, and being accompanied with His Royall, not His Martiall Attendance, return to His two Houses of Parliament, and there reside with them. And for the better security of all His Majesties Subjects, He proposeth that He with His said two Houses immediately upon His coming to *Westminster* will passe an Act of Oblivion and free pardon, and where His Majesty will further do whatsoever they will advise Him

Him for the good and peace of this Kingdom. And as for the Kingdom of *Scotland* His Majesty hath made no mention of it here, in regard of the great losse of time which must now be spent in expecting an Answer from thence, but declares that, immediately upon His comming to *Westminster,* He will apply Himself to give them all satisfaction touching that Kingdome. If His Majesty could possibly doubt the successe of this offer, He could use many arguments to perswade them to it ; but shall only insist on that great One of giving an instant Peace to these afflicted Kingdoms.

Given at our Court at Oxford, *the* 23 *of* March, 1645.

For the Speaker of the House of Peers pro tempore, *to be Communicated to the two Houses of Parlia-*
liament at Westminster.

AS God said, *what could I have done more for my vineyard which I have not done ?* so may this good Prince say, what could I have offered more for the *Peace* of my afflicted People, which I have not offered ? These men (that will accept of nothing) tell the world in their late *Declaration*, that themselves *had made Application to Him for Peace, no lesse then seven times (scil.* in seven years.) But the world hath now seen, that His Majesty hath made *Applications* to them for the same thing, no lesse then *ten times* in lesse then four moneths, and in another *form* and *stile* too, then theirs were to Him, and not one word in Answer can He get from them ; yea for Peace sake He offers to venture Himself among them, but they'l none of Him, He would *come to His owne* (as they call themselves) *but His own will not receive Him*.

It shall not be amisse, if the world, to whom the appeal is made, shall call to minde in this place, some few of their many former solemne *professions* which are directly contradicted by these their present behaviours ; let their *Protestation* or *Declara-*

G *tion*

tion of Octob. 22. 1642. be read, and therein they will finde these expressions.

We the Lords and Commons in this present Parliament Assembled, doe in the presence of Almighty God, for the satisfaction of our Consciences; and discharge of that great trust which lies upon us, make this Protestation and Declaration to this Kingdome and Nation, and to the whole World, that no private passion or respect, no evill intention to His Majesties Person, no designe to the prejudice of His just Honour and Authority ingaged us to raise forces, and take up Armes, &c.

And againe,

We professe from our very Hearts and Souls, our Loyalty and Obedience to His Crown; readinesse and resolution to defend His Person, and support His Estate with our lives and fortunes, to the uttermost of our power.

Againe,

We professe, we desire nothing from His Majesty, but that He would returne in Peace to His Parliament.

And againe,

We professe in the sight of Almighty God, which is the strongest obligation that a Christian, and the most solemne publicke faith, which any such State as a Parliament can give; that we would receive Him with all Honour, yeild Him all true obedience and subjection, and faithfully endeavour to defend His Person and Estate from all danger, and to the utmost of our power to stablish Him, and His people all the blessings of a most Glorious and Happy Raign, &c.

Surely they, who shall compare these Professions, with the present Carriages of them that made them, will conclude them the vilest *Atheists* that ever lived; and beleeve that they used these *Protestations* only, to gull and seduce the well meaning *Common-people*, that so they might cheat them of their Monies, and engage them with themselves in wayes of *Treason, Bloud* and *Rebellion*, to the destruction of their *Religion, King* and *Country*: But *verily there is a God that judgeth the Earth, and that these mockers of Him shall feel ere long, for the day of their Calamity is at Hand, and the things that are comming upon them make hast.*

Wel, his Maj. after he had sent this His tenth Message for Peace, &, waited another month and more, for an Answer thereof, having

under-

understood by their former unworthy *Paper* of the 13 of *Janu.* (and being confirmed also, by their silence to all His Profers) that no admittance would be granted to Him, though He came alone; for as at the approach of Christ, the *Devill raged* and *tore* the party possessed; so did jealousies and guilty fears *rend* and *torment* them at the Apprehension of His presence, or accesse unto them; and therefore, till He should first consent to such *Propositions* as they would at their further leasure send unto Him; He must not come near them, unlesse He be brought by the *Souldiers* before them, as Christ was into the *High Priests Hall,* viz. in the nature of a *Prisoner :* & indeed to this purpose, while they think to delude Him, still with a further expectation of *Propositions* (which they never meant should be seen at *Oxford;*) they send thither as fast as they can, all their Armies and Bands of Souldiers, with *Guns* and *Swords,* and *Staves for to take Him ;* concluding with themselves, that He would surely fall into the Hand of their *Strong ones,* and could not possibly escape them : But God was too hard for them, He seeing their mischeivous intentions, inclined the Heart of His Majesty to goe, and protected Him safe in going to the *Scottish Army :* where so soon as He came, (that all might see His desires of Peace, were not capable of abatement) He falls againe to His old work of soliciting for the same ; and offers to these unreasonable men, all that ever was desired to give them content : He refers to them and their Divines *the setling of Religion* ; He consents the *Militia* to be *at their disposall,* His Forces to be *disbanded,* His Townes and Garrisons *dismantled* and deserted, and what ever else had been formerly in dispute betwixt them ; and if these would not be now accepted, becauseoffered by Him, (though formerly desired by them) He wills them to send their long promised Propositions, or at least, those of them which were agreed upon, being resolved to comply in every thing, as shall but appear to Him, to be for His *Subjects* happinesse : And notwithstanding all the contempts they had shewn *Him,* and affronts put upon *Him* ; *He* still hath, or desires to have so good an opinion of them, that *He* will not question their good acceptation of these His offers, since He makes no conditions with them for Himselfe, but is content to leave His own *Honour* and *Lawfull* Rights, solely to their care and gratitude to

main-

maintain unto Him : Let all men read (without admiration if they can at the Kings Chriftianity and goodneffe) this which follows : how in very deed He *yeilds up His will and Affections, His Reafon, Judgment,* and all for the *obtaining a good peace or accommodation* with thefe Stubborn men unto His poor and afflicted people.

His Majesties eleventh Meſſage.

CHARLS R.

HIs Majefty having underftood from both His Houfes of Parliament, that it was not fafe for him to come to *London* (whither he had purpofed to repair, if fo he might, by their advice to do whatfoever may be beft for the good and peace of thefe Kingdoms) untill he fhall firft give his confent to fuch Propofitions, as were to be prefented to him from them : And being certainly informed that the Armies were marching fo faft up to *Oxford*, and made that no fit place for Treating, did refolve to withdraw himfelf hither, only to fecure his own Perfon, and with no intention to continue this War any longer, or to make any divifion between his two Kingdoms, but to give fuch contentment to both, as, by the bleffing of God, he might fee a happy and wel-grounded Peace, thereby to bring Profperity to thefe Kingdoms, anfwerable to the beft times of his Progenitors.

And fince the fetling of Religion ought to be the chiefeft care of all Councels, his Majefty moft earneftly and heartily recommends to his two Houfes of Parliament all the waies and means poffible, for fpeedy finifhing this pious & neceffary work ; and particularly, that they take the advice of the Divines of both Kingdoms affembled at
Weftminfter.

*Westminster.*Likewise concerning the *Militia* of *England,*
for fecuring his people againft all pretenfions of danger,
his Majefty is pleafed to have it fetled as was offered at
the Treaty at *Uxbridge*; all the Perfons being to be named for the Truft by the two Houfes of the Parliament
of *England,* for the fpace of feven years, and after the
expiring of that term, that it be regulated as fhall be a-
greed upon by his Majefty and his two Houfes of Parliament.

And the like for the Kingdom of *Scotland.*

Concerning the Wars in *Ireland,* his Majefty will do
whatfoever is poffible for him, to give full fatisfaction
therein.

And if thefe be not fatisfactory, his Majefty then defires that all fuch of the Propofitions as are already a-
greed upon by both Kingdoms may be fpeedily fent unto him; his Majefty being refolved to comply with his
Parliament in every thing that fhall be for the happineffe
of his Subjects, and for the removing of all unhappy differences, which have produced fo many fad effects.

His Majefty having made thefe offers, he will neither
queftion the thankfull acceptation of them; nor doth he
doubt but that his two Kingdoms will be carefull to
maintain him in his Honour, and in his juft and lawfull
Rights, which is the only way to make a happy compo-
fure of thefe unnaturall Divifions. And likewife will
think upon a folid way of conferving the Peace between
the two Kingdoms for time to come. And will take a
fpeedy courfe for eafing and quieting his afflicted people
by fatisfying the Publike debts, by disbanding of all
Armies, and whatfoever elfe fhall be judged conducible
to that end: that fo, all hinderances being removed, he
may return to his Parliament with mutuall comfort.

Southwell, *May* 18. 1646.

POST-SCRIPT.

*HIs Majesty being desirous to shun the further effusion of
bloud, and to evidence His reall intentions to Peace, is
willing that His Forces in, and about Oxford be disbanded,
and the fortifications of the City dismantled, they receiving
honourable conditions. Which being granted to the Town
and Forces there, His Majesty will give the like order to the
rest of the Garrisons.*

*For the Speaker of the House of Peers pro tempore,
To be Communicated to the two Houses of Parliament at* Westminster, *and the Commissioners of
the Parliament of* Scotland.

THis Message from His Majesty out of the *Scots* Quarters,
though as full of *Grace* as could be wished, found as little
respect as any of the former, and was thought as unworthy of an
Answer; for indeed it spake (to their great grief) the escape of
that rich *prey* which was already swallowed in their Expectations, yea and an impossibility of getting it into their reach again
with so little cost and pains as they hoped before to be possessed
of it: for they conceived the frugall *Scot* was not like to part
with his *Liege Lord,* and native King for nothing; nor be so easily beaten from hence to their own home, as was intended they
should have been, so soon as the Kings Person had been seized on
at *Oxford:* for His Majesties Presence, like the Glorious Sun,
drew thousands of Eyes upon His Country-men, and would have
fetch'd as many hearts and hands to their Assistance, had they
but then stood up in defence of Him. This they at *Westminster*
well knew, and hereupon saw, that a kind of necessity lay on
them, to shuffle again, and after another fashion then before was
purposed: to play the *Foxes* in stead of the *Lions* with their *dear
Brethren:* and therefore they begin at last to think of doing that,
which till now they never intended, though often promised; even
of sending *Propositions* to the King: which on *July* 24. (two
                                                           months

months after their receipt of this last Message of *May* 18.) arived at Him, under the name of *Propositions for Peace*: but the contrivers of them, had in their Provident care made them so perfectly *monstrous* and *unreasonable*, that themselves remained sure still of being out of all danger of Effecting Peace by them : in very deed they were only used to gain time and opportunity to recover their lost *prey*, and to delude the *Scots*, who were not then so well acquainted with their spirits, as (perhaps) since they have been, or at least may be, before a period be put to these *troubles*. Those *Propositions* of theirs were as tedious as senseless, for what they wanted in *reason*, was made up in *words*, they have been published already, and therefore we shall not here trouble the Reader with them, there be *Copies* enow extant of them, which whosoever views, will think the Kingdom might have imployed their many hundred thousand pounds better, then in maintaining so many men, and so many Armies so many months together, in doing nothing but making such uncouth *Propositions*. By this insuing Message of his Majesty in Answer to them, within a week after His receipt of them, the world (were it ignorant of them) might have a glimpse of what *kind* they were, and of what *spirit* those that sent them.

His *Majesties* twelfth *Message*.

CHARLES R.

THe Propositions tendered to His Majesty by the Commissioners from the Lords and Commons Assembled in the Parliament of *England* at *Westminster*, and the Commissioners of the Parliament of *Scotland*, (to which the Houses of Parliament have taken twice so many Monthes for deliberation, as they have assigned dayes for his Majesties Answer) do import so great alterations in Government, both in Church and Kingdome, as it is very difficult to return a particular and positive Answer before a full debate, wherein

wherein thefe Propofitions and the neceffary explanations, true fenfe and reafons thereof be rightly weighed
and underftood, and that his Majefty upon a full view
of the whole Propofitions may know what is left, as
well as what is taken away and changed, In all which
he finds (upon difcourfe with the faid Commiffioners
that they are fo bound up from any capacity, either to
give reafons for the demands they bring, or to give ear
to fuch defires as his Majefty is to propound, as it is
impoffible for him to give fuch a prefent judgement of,
& Anfwer to thefe Propofitions, whereby he can Anfwer
to God that a fafe and well-grounded peace will enfue
(which is evident to all the world can never be, unleffe
the juft power of the Crown, as well as the freedome and
propriety of the Subject, with the juft liberty and priviledges of the Parliament be likewife fetled) To which
end his Majefty defires and propofeth to come to *London*; or any of his houfes thereabouts upon the publick
faith, and fecurity of the two houfes of Parliament, and
the Scotch Commiffioners, That he fhall be there with
freedome, honour, and fafety, whereby his perfonall
prefence he may not only raife a mutuall confidence betwixt him and his people, but alfo have thefe doubts
cleared, and thefe difficulties explained unto him; which
he now conceives to be deftructive to his juft regall power, if he fhall give a ful confent to thefe Propofitions as
they now ftand.

As likewife, that he make known to them, fuch his
reafonable demands as he is moft affured will be very
much conducible to that Peace, which all good men
defire and pray for, by the fetling of Religion, the juft
priviledges of Parliament, with the freedom and propriety of the Subject; and his Majefty affures them that

as

as he can never condiscend unto what is absolutely destructive to that just power, which by the laws of God
and the Land he is born unto; So he wil cheerfully grant,
and give his assent unto all such Bills, at the desire of his
two Houses, or reasonable demands for *Scotland,* which
shall be really for the good and Peace of his people, not
having regard to his own particular (much lesse of any
bodies else) in respect of the happinesse of these Kingdomes. Wherefore his Majesty conjures them as Christians, as Subjects, and as men who desire to leave a good
name behind them, that they will so receive and make
use of this Answer, that all issues of bloud may be stopped, and these unhappy distractions peaceably setled.

Newcastle, August 1. 1646.

POST-SCRIPT.

UPon assurance of a happy agreement, His Majesty will
immediately send for the Prince His Son, absolutely ex-
pecting His perfect Obedience to return into this Kingdom.

To the Speaker of the House of Peers
pro tempore, to be communicated.

BY this Message the Readers may observe, that the contrivers
of those *Propositions,* though themselves were many, and had
imployed all their craft, (which was not little). 8 Months together (as they pretended) in the framing of them, yet were perswaded (as it seems) that His Majesty alone, in regard of His
clear *wisdome, sincerity,* and *honesty* of Heart; was able in three
or four dayes to Answer them fully; and therefore they assigned
him no longer time to deliberate on them : or else they supposed
that His Maj. in His eagernesse of minde to obtain *Peace,*so oft &
earnestly writ for by Him, would blindly and suddainly consent
without more adoe, to what ever (on that condition) they asked

H   of of Him : for as crafty Chapmen will enhaunse the price (beyond all reason) of that Commodity they have to sell, when they see a Customer fond of it ; so did these men deal with their King : He had fully manifested a most fervent desire of procuring quiet to His people, by His many *Messages* & large *Offers*, wherein He had shewed a readinesse to yeild up His own *Rights*, or (to speak in their phrase) *His will* and *Affections, yea, and His Reason and Judgement too*, for the purchase of it : So it were reall and good : Whereupon, perhaps they fancied that He would not stick to resigne up His *Conscience* also, (upon their demand) together with the *Rights* of His *Crown* (to which He was born) and the *trust* committed to Him by God and the Law, over the *lives* and *Estates* of all His Subjects, into those Hands which have been excercised in nothing this seven years, but *Bloud, Rapine*, and *Oppression*, without any probability of recovering the same againe to Himselfe, or His successors.

For, indeed they are now come to that pitch of the *pinacle*, that unlesse the King will condescend to *cast Himself down*, to destroy himself, and to ruine *Monarchy*, no concessions of His shall please them, nor shall his many *Messages* and large *offers* obtaine *peace* from them unto his people ; who may themselves judge of what kinde it would be, (by that experience they have had of them already) if the King should yeild so far, as to lay down his life and Crown for the purchase.

But God be thanked, our King is no *Child*, nor false *Shepherd* ; but a *man after Gods own Heart*, and a very *Moses*, though meeke and patient to admiration in his own case, (throughout all his dealings with this stif-necked and rebellious generation;) yet most *valiant* and *magnanimous* in the Cause of God, and most faithfull in the discharge of that trust reposed in Him : our Saviour would rather suffer himself to be *no Man*, then yeild himself to be *no King* ; he would rather part with his *life*, then his *Kingship*, and so will our Soveraign : and therefore our God (we trust) will preserve both, for the further Happinesse, yet of this Church and Nation.

But let's observe His Majesties goodnesse towards these men, in this His Message or Answer to their *Propositions* ; He was ashamed (as seemeth) that the world should take full notice of
their

their impiety and unreasonablenesse in them ; and therefore
was pleased to shadow the same (in a measure) from the
worlds eye, by impleading the *difficulty of understanding* the said
Propositions for want of *necessary explanations*, as if there had been,
or might haply be more *Justice* and *Reason* in them, then was apparent (when indeed there was more *mischeife* then could be
easily beleeved:) And this he alledgeth as the cause of his not returning *particular Answers* to them ; and in truth, there is much
ambiguity and darknesse in them, which the Contrivers were stu-
dious and carefull to leave in their composing of them, that thereby themselves might still have evasions, and occasions to raise
cavills, what ever His Majesties Answer should be unto them : to
which end also they were provident to Bind up their *Commissioners* tongues from speaking any such word in way of discourse,
as might discover to the King their further meanings.

Wherefore his Majesty finding it impossible to returne such a
plenary Answer, as in His Conscience might be justifiable in
Gods sight, or conductive to a safe and well-grounded peace ; he
proposeth again his *own comming to London*, to treat with them,
and (for the avoiding of all mistakes) to *hear them explaine their
own meanings* ; and ingages himself to give his *cheerfull assent
to all such Bills as shall be really to the good and peace of His people*,
and to prefer *the Happinesse of this Kingdome, before His own particular* ; and as a mean to work a confidence in them, of His
own sincerity in these things; he offers again to trust them with
no lesse then his *own Person* ; and conjures them, *as they are Christians, as they are Subjects*, and *as they are men, who desire to leave a
good name behinde them, so to receive, & make use of this His Answer,
that all issues of Bloud may be stopped, and these unhappy distractions
peaceably setled.*

But (as appears) neither the *Dignity* of *Christians*, the *Duty* of
Subjects, nor the *Credit* of a *good Name* will prevaile with them,
any more then his Majesties former Messages and Intreaties had
done ; for they had (as it seemes) renounced and rejected them
all before hand, and therefore without taking any notice of
this *Conjuration* of their Soveraign, or of any thing else which he
had writ unto them in the whole Message ; they go on silently,
and resolutely, in that way which themselves had chosen.

which His Majesty observing after some months patient expe-
ctance, bent His thoughts to the making some *particular Answers*
to the fore-mentioned *Propositions*, desiring (if possible) to give
them content : but upon His most serious consideration on them,
He found that He did but labour in vain, for He could not speak
so unto them, but some (who lay in wait for that purpose) would
mis-construe and pervert His sayings to a contrary sence, unlesse
Himself were present among them to *paraphrase upon his owne*
Words, and explain His meaning, wherefore He hoping that Gods
grace and spirit might at last (peradventure) have some footing
in their minds, He rather chuseth to propose again by another
Message (five months after the former) His *own coming unto them*,
and renues His *former offers*, discovering thereby that notwithstanding their transcendent neglects and contempts of Him, yet
He was still as constant in His *good intentions* to them, as they
were in their *ill resolutions* against Him : His words are these.

His Majesties thirteenth Message.

CHARLS R.

HIs Majesties thoughts being alwaies sincerely
bent to the Peace of His Kingdoms, was & will
be ever desirous to take all waies which might
the most cleerly make appear the candour of His intentions to His people. And to this end, could find no better way then to propose a Personall free debate with His
two Houses of Parliament upon all the present differences. Yet finding very much against His expectations,
that this offer was laid aside, His Majesty bent all His
thoughts to make His intentions fully known by a particular Answer to the Propositions delivered to Him in
the name of both Kingdomes, 24. *July* last. But the
more He endeavoured it, He more plainly saw that any
Answer He could make would be subject to mis-infor-
mations

mations and mif-conftructions, which upon His owne Paraphrafes and Explanations He is moft confident will give fo good fatisfaction, as would doubtleffe caufe a happy and lafting Peace. Left therefore that good intentions may produce ill effects, His Majefty again proposeth, and defires again to come to *London,* or any of His Houfes thereabouts, upon the Publike Faith and Security of His two Houfes of Parliament, and the Scotch Commiffioners, that He fhall be there with Honour, Freedome, and Safety: Where, by His Perfonall Prefence, He may not only raife a mutuall confidence betwixt Him and His People, but alfo have thofe doubts cleared, and thofe difficulties explained to Him, without which He cannot (but with the aforefaid mifchievous inconveniencies) give a particular Anfwer to the Propofitions: And with which He doubts not, but fo to manifeft His reall intentions for the fetling of Religion, the juft priviledges of Parliament, with the Freedome and Property of the Subject, that it fhall not be in the power of wicked and malicious men to hinder the eftablifhing of that firm Peace which all honeft men defire. Affuring them, as He will make no other Demands but fuch as He believes confidently to be juft, and much conducing to the Tranquility of the People: So He will be moft willing to condefcend to them in whatfoever fhall be really for their good and happineffe. Not doubting likewife but you will alfo have a due regard to maintain the juft Power of the Crown, according to your many Proteftations and profeffions. For certainly, except King and People have reciprocall care each of other, neither can be happy.

To conclude, 'tis your *King* who defires to be heard, (the which, if refufed to a Subject by a King, he would

be

be thought a Tyrant for it) and for that end which all men professe to desire. Wherefore His Majesty conjures you, as you desire to shew your selves really what you professe, even as you are good Christians and Subjects, that you wil accept this His Offer, which He is confident God will so blesse, that it will be the readiest means by which these Kingdoms may again become a comfort to their Friends, and a terrour to their Enemies.

Newcastle, 20. Decemb. 1646.

> *To the Speaker of the House of Peers* pro tempore, *to be communicated to the two Houses of Parliament at* Westminster, *and to the Commissioners of the Parliament of* Scotland.

WHat man can read without tears, these *pathetick* desires and expressions of His Soveraigne, only *to be Heard,* and that but *to Speak* and plead by word of mouth, for the peace and tranquility of His people, sith His many *Messages* by writing (to this purpose) were not regarded? sure these Persons have hearts *harder then the neither Mil-stone,* they have forgot themselves to be, either *Christians, Subjects,* or *men;* but doubtlesse the time will come, when *they,* who thus stop their ears at the requests of their King, shall themselves cry, *and not be heard,* and no man shall pity them. His Majesty we see, refuses nothing which may tend to the *setling of Religion, the freedom of Parliament,* and *property of the Subjects:* He denies no pardon, security, or indemnity, to these His Enemies, (that *will not have Him to reign over them*) if they would accept it: His own *rights* He'll refer to them to be setled, as may be to the Kingdoms good, as to His own; in a probable continuation of Gods blessing upon the same, as upon himself: His *Person* He offers to their *trust,* and the just *power* of His Crown to their *care;* nor is He willing so much as to doubt of their due regard in maintaining the same unto Him, according to their many Protestations and professions.

And nothing doth He desire for Himself (in lieu of all this) but
only

only leave to *speak*, liberty to be *heard*, which Himself in His prosperity *never denied to the meanest Person*, though the greatest Malefactor : Let all the world with admiration think upon it, and judge in the case, what Prince can offer more, then He hath done ? or what man can desire lesse ? what Christian spirit doth not *rise* to see Piety and Majesty thus slighted, and despised ? what Subjects bloud doth not *boyle* to hear his Soveraigne forced for the purchase of so *little*, to offer so *much* unto His own *Vassals*, and yet be repulsed and rejected by them ? should *Turks* and *Heathens* behold this, they would be inraged ; could the inferiour *Creatures* apprehend it, even they would grow furious at it : surely, this is, and may be, a matter of astonishment to the whole earth, for (as the Prophet saies) *Passe over the Isles, send to other Lands, inquire of all Nations*, search all stories of former and later times, consider diligently, and *see well, if there be, or ever were any such thing*, or ever the like heard of, from the beginning of time : Did ever people thus exclude their King, or thus vilely use him ? set but that act of the Jews aside against our Saviour, and this example may be affirmed to be *Sans parallel:* never did Subjects make larger *protestations* and *professions* of love and duty, and never could *Devils* go more contrary unto the same then these *men* have done : let but *those their words* already quoted (upon the tenth Message) be seriously considered on, and of necessity it will be concluded, that *Hell* is not more opposite to *Heaven*, nor *darknesse* to *light*, then their *carriages* are, and have been unto those *expressions* : and so it seems 'tis resolved they shall be still, for His Majesties conjuring them *to shew themselves really to be what they professed*, no whit moves them to shew themselves any other then they *really are :* now they have catch'd the fish, cheated the people, inslaved the Nation, got their owne ends, the power into their hands to keep all men under, they may fling away their *baits*, throw off their *vizards*, cast aside their *disguises*, and appear freely in their proper shapes and colours : All their solemn *Protestations* and *professions* were of the same nature and tenure, with their *solemn League and Covenant*, which (as *Martin* himself, one of their prime birds, openly saies) *was not intended to be everlastingly kept ;* the causes of making them being but as the grounds of *striking that, meerly occasionall, for the joyning in a War to*

suppresse

suppresse the Common Enemy (for so now they call the King) and *He being suppressed,*what are the *Protestations* and *professions* come to be, but as the *Covenant* it self is, only *like an Almanack of last year,* of no more regard or estimation,witnesse *Hen. Martin, p.11.* of *Indepency of* England *maintain'd against the claim of the Scotch Commissioners.*

In vain therefore did His Majesty (by mentioning their former *Protestations* and *professions)* put them in mind of things out of date ; and to as little purpose did He again desire to come to *London in Safety and Honour,* for they could not hear on that side ; indeed they were otherwise busied at that time, even truck-ing to get Him into their power another way, then that was which He propounded : for have Him they would, they were re-solved on that, what ere it cost them ; and they meant to receive Him too, but not in that manner as He desired, not *with Safety,* but *into* safe custody, from injoying *his Liberty;*not *with Honour to Him,*but *in triumph* to themselves ; not as their *Prince,*but as their *Prisoner :* even directly as the Jews at length received Christ, not as the *gift* of his own *free love,* but as the *price* of their own *base mony ;* So that His Majesty saw ere long (after His sending the last Message) a perfect frustration, both of it, and all His former, and that Himself had somewhat else to do, beside begging *peace* unto His people, and *Liberty of Speech* unto Himself : for free-dome of Conscience to serve God,after the legall and established way of the true *Protestant English Church,* is now denied Him, as an additionall punishment to His outward restraint, which now also is layed upon Him, for being so importunate for His Subjects freedome from *war* and *pressures.*

Holdenby is the place of His inclosement, He was *carried* thi-ther, as *Christ into the wildernesse to be tempted ;* and kept there with as much care from *spirituall* food, as Christ was from *bodily,* and that not forty daies together only, but above three times forty ; and under temptations all the while : Master *Marshall and his fellow Minister* being chose out to act Satans part upon Him : for having been so specially instrumentall in destroying the Souls of *His* People, and in stirring them up to kill each other, they were judged the fittest in the *whole Legion* to assault Him : And all the helps to vexation and trouble, that the *Heads at West-*

minster

minster could think upon, thefe *Tempters* had for their advantage : But the *Spirit of God* was fo ftrong in this *Royall Champion,* that *they were* not able to ftand before *Him,* nor *to refift the wifdome and Learning by which He fpake,* infomuch that *as they* in the Gofpel were forced to confeffe, whether they would or no, *that Chrift was the Son of God,* though before they had laboured to obfcure him : fo were thefe, even compelled againft their own wills to acknowledge in fecret, among their friends, that *the King was a moft able, judicious Prince, and the wifeft man in all His Kingdoms,* clean contrary to that, which they had often blattered in Pulpits againft Him before the People. And Mafter *Marſhall* at laft, was fo tormented with His Majefties *Divinity* and *Reafon,* by being fo neer him, that he wifhed to be in the *Herd* again (his more proper place) where he was likely to effect more mifchief, and therefore befought his Mafters at *Weſtminſter,* to be recall'd from *Holdenby,* or fent no more thither.

But though His Majefty was able enough of *Himfelf* to encounter thefe, yet for *the better exercife of His Confcience* in pious duties, and for the further *clearing of His judgment concerning the prefent differences,* He defires to have *two* from out of *twelve* of His own *Chaplains* to attend upon Him, which He defires His *two Houſes* to make choice of, and fend to Him ; in thefe words,

His Majeſties fourteenth Meſſage.

His Majeſties gracious Meſſage to both Houſes of Parliament, concerning His Chaplains.

SInce I have never diffembled, nor hid my Confcience, and that I am not yet fatisfied with the alteration of Religion, to which you defire my confent, I will not yet lofe time in giving reafons, which are too obvious to every body, why it is fit for me to be attended by fome of my Chaplains, whofe opinions, as Clergy men, I efteem and reverence ; not only for the exercife of my Confcience, but alfo for clearing of my

I

judgment

judgment concerning the present differences in Religion; as I have at full declared to Master *Marshall* and his *Fellow-Minister:* having shewed them, that it is the best and likeliest means of giving me satisfaction, which without it I cannot have in these times: Whereby the distractions of this Church may be the better setled. Wherefore I desire that, at least, two of these *Reverend Divines,* whose names I have here set down, may have free liberty to wait upon me, for the discharge of their duty unto me , according to their function.

CHARLS R.

Holdenby, 17. *Febr.* 1646.

B. *London.*	D. *Sanderson.*
B. *Salisbury.*	D. *Baily.*
B. *Peterborough.*	D. *Heywood.*
D. *Shelden,* Clerk of my Closet.	D. *Beale.*
	D. *Fuller.*
D. *Marsh,* Deane of York.	D. *Hammond.*
	D. *Taylor.*

For the Speaker of the House of Peers pro tempore, *to be communicated,* &c.

THe *matter* of this *Message* or thing desired therein, is *freedome of Conscience,* and the *necessary means to serve God,* according to the Doctrine and way of the *English Church.*

The *Person* from whom the request comes, is the King of this Nation, the *Supreamest Defender* under God upon Earth of the *Protestant Faith,* who never denied the exercise of it to any creature. And the *Men* to whom the same is sent, are the most open *Protesters* that ever were for freedome and Liberty in this kind, and that to all men: and the most violent exclaimers against those that restrain any: yea and they are such beside as call themselves

selves His Majesties *most Humble and Loyall Subjects*: therefore it may be thought a thing impoſſible, that this requeſt ſhould not be granted; ſpecially too,if we do but obſerve how CHARLS R. appears below, ſubmiſſively at the bottome, (now He moves for a private matter, and as a Chriſtian) which is wont alway when He writes about *publike* and *Kingly Affairs* to ſtand above, in its proper place, before the beginning.

Oh but theſe are rare men, they never denied themſelves yet, but the King ever, it cannot be ſaid to this day, that they have yeilded to Him, in the leaſt particular, ſince they there ſat, and ſhould they begin now to break their old wont ? ſo they might ſeem to halt in their reſolved courſe, and He might haply flatter Himſelf too much in hoping they meant to look towards Him : wherefore though all men elſe, have leave to be of what Religion they *liſt*,& to worſhip God after what faſhion they *pleaſe*;yet He for His part ſhall not be ſuffered to have the means to ſerve him the true way, nor to heare the Doctrine of that Church which themſelves as well as He, were baptized into, and have proteſted to maintain : and thereupon having practiſed long to hold their peace to His other Meſſages, they reſolve upon ſilence to this alſo, and return nothing : But His Majeſty being wel (and too wel) acquainted with ſuch uſage from their hands, and being as *patient*, as they were *peeviſh* : as unwearied in *good*, as they in *evill*, doth in a moſt calm and Chriſtian manner renew His requeſt for the ſame thing ſeventeen daies after,in theſe words :

His *Majeſties fifteenth Meſſage.*

His *Majeſties ſecond Meſſage to both Houſes of Parliament, concerning His Chaplains.*

IT being now ſeventeen daies ſince I wrote to you from hence, and not yet receiving any Anſwer to what I then deſired, I cannot but now again renew the ſame unto you. And indeed concerning any thing but the neceſſary duty of a Chriſtian, I would not thus

at

at this time trouble you with any of my defires. But my being attended with fome of my Chaplains, whom I efteem and reverence, is fo neceffary for me, even confidering my prefent condition, whether it be in relation to my confcience, or a happy fetlement of the prefent diftractions in Religion, that I will flight divers kinds of cenfures, rather then not to obtain what I demand ; nor fhall I do you the wrong, as in this, to doubt the obtaining of my wifh, it being totally grounded upon reafon. For defiring you to confider (not thinking it needfull to mention) the divers reafons, which no Chriftian can be ignorant of, for point of confcience, I muft affure you that I cannot, as I ought, take in confideration thofe alterations in Religion, which have and will be offered unto me, without fuch help as I defire ; becaufe I can never judge rightly of, or be altered in, any thing of my opinion, fo long as any ordinary way of finding out the truth is denied me ; but when this is granted me, I promife you faithfully not to ftrive for victory in Argument, but to feek and fubmit to Truth (according to that judgment which God hath given me) alwaies holding it my beft and greateft conqueft to give contentment to my two Houfes of Parliament in all things, which, I conceive, not to be againft my confcience or honour ; not doubting likewife but that you will be ready to fatisfie me in reafonable things, as I hope to find in this particular concerning the attendance of my Chaplains upon me.

    CHARLS R.

Holdenby, 6. *March,* 1646.

    For the Speaker of the Houfe of Peers pro tempore, *to be Communicated to the two Houfes of Parliament at* Weftminfter.

AS an evill man out of the evill treasure of his heart, bringeth forth evill things; such are causlesse Jealousies, railing Accusations, and evill surmizings against the *good*: So a *good man out of the good treasure of his heart, bringeth forth good things*: such are favourable opinions, meek expressions, and charitable constructions; and from hence it was that His Majesty writes in this manner *to*, and *of* these men: as if He still hoped there might possibly be some good sparks of *grace, nature*, or *manners* in them: for as they cannot believe Him to be *so good, as He is*: so He cannot yet fancy them *so bad, as they be*, and mean to prove themselves: He tels them, in this His Message, that *He would not have troubled them at this time, with any of His desires, did not this particular concern the necessary duty of a Christian, and relate so neerly to His Conscience*: conceiving (as it seems)that they would be the more *inclinable* in this regard, whereas (alas) their dispositions are to be the more *averse*: their aimes being (as hath appeared by all their dealings) *to destroy His Conscience*, and to keep Him from serving God at all: Have they not often said unto Him in their language,(*Go serve other Gods?*)they would at least occasion a strangenesse, betwixt His God and Him: that God might be further off from His assistance, and so His spirit might sink more under the Burdens which they lay upon Him: they have not forgot *Balaams* project against the *Israelites*, and fain would they put it in practice upon their King: for they well see, they shall never be able to do Him the mischief they intend, while God is with Him, in this mighty manner to guide and strengthen Him: and therefore they must first endevour to bring Him out with His God; and since, by all their compulsions and temptations they cannot prevail to drive Him upon *commissions* of evill, they would fain force Him to be guilty of some *omissions* of good, and keep Him from performing the *necessary duties of a Christian*, and therefore they will not suffer Him to injoy the *service of His own Chaplains*.

Again, His Majesty desires to have *their service*, as means *relating to an happy setlement of the present distractions in Religion*, and *as necessary helps to His Conscience in the Consideration of those Alterations in the same, which had been already, and He knew would still be offered unto Him*: and this He urgeth as another Argu-

ment

ment of His wish or desire, and it being *totally grounded upon Reason,* He saies *He doubts not to obtain it from them.*

But His Majesty hath since found, that His *Charity* was much mistaken in this too : and indeed 'tis the greatest wrong that ere He did them, *His thinking so well of them,* as to conceive Himself likely to obtain any of His *requests* at their hands, because *grounded upon Reason* ; or to hope for any helps from their allowance, towards the setlement of the present distractions in Religion : for should they yeild to undoe their own work ? did not they make all these distractions in Church and State ? were any of them in being before they sat ? do they not live by them ? could they injoy their power, and Lord it as they do, if things were setled in *Religion* ? would not all things return to their proper chanels, if *that* were well composed ? no, no, if these be the Kings ends of desiring His Chaplains, He must learn to know (at length) that they have more subtilty, and self-love in them, then to listen to Him. Let Him rest contented therefore in this particular, He must enter the lists, *and fight the Bataile himself alone* ; for they are resolved to put Him to it, *of His friends,* (or people) *there shall be none with Him* ; no not so much as one of *His own Chaplains :* And whereas He promises *not to strive for victory in Argument, but to seek and submit to Truth :* He must know, that they do not look for victory that way against Him, yet they mean to have it too, & that without any *seeking* or *submitting to truth* at all for it.

And He may for His part (if He please) hold it His best and greatest conquest, *to give contentment to His two Houses of Parliament in all things that are not against His Conscience and Honour :* yet they who are the domineering faction in His *two Houses,* (and call themselves the Parliament) will still hold it *their best and greatest conquest,* to discontent and vex His spirit : nor will they think their *Conquest* compleat, unlesse they can prevail, to inforce some breaches upon *His Conscience and Honour :* and therefore He may even cease from henceforth, thus to fancy any readinesse in them, to satisfie His desires in *any reasonable thing,* for they will not do it in this poor particular, concerning *the Attendance of His Chaplains* upon Him.

These, these are the men that contemn God, that say in their hearts, *Tush, God seeth not :* nor doth he regard such things, nor

will

will He ever require an account for them : *But thou dost see,* and thou hast seen *(O Lord) for thou beholdest mischief and spight to requite it with thine hand,* O keep not long silence therefore, be not far off from thine Anointed ; Stir up thy self, and awake to his Judgment, and unto His cause, *thou art his God, thou* (alone) *art his Lord ;* Judge thou for Him according to thy righteousnesse, and let not these miscreant men triumph any longer over Him, let them not say in their hearts, *Ah ! so would we have it.* Let them not say, we have swallowed him up, let them be ashamed and brought to confusion together that rejoice at his hurt, yea let them be cloathed with shame and dishonour that magnifie themselves against Him : but let them shout for joy, and ever have cause to be glad, that favour His righteous cause, yea let them say continually, *Let the Lord be magnified which hath pleasure in the prosperity of His servant.* Amen, Amen.

His Majesty at last (having waited two months for Answer) was sufficiently informed by their silence, how vainly He laboured in soliciting for His *Chaplains,* and thereupon forbears to be further importunate in that businesse ; it concerned His own particular *self* and *comfort,* and He can more easily desist in pursuing a thing of *that* nature ; then in seeking for a blessing which more immediately concerns His people, and therefore though His request for *Peace* had been rejected thirteen times already, in lesse then thirteen months, yet He cannot hold from renewing that : yea though they had frustrated His expectation a long time, in not sending such Propositions as they had promised, or given Him hopes to receive, for His more full and clear understanding their sence in the former, and did also keep His Person, in so unworthy, so unheard of, and so provocative a Condition, as might have swell'd with stoutnesse the mildest heart, and awaken'd *passion* (had it not been dead) in a very Martyr, yet with the greatest meeknesse and sweetnesse of stile that can be imagined doth He write unto them again, and sends most gracious Answers to their former unreasonable *Propositions,* after He had diligently endevoured and studied divers moneths how to make them such, *as (salva conscientia) might be most agreeable to the likings of His Parliaments.* His words are these,

His

His Majesties sixteenth Message.

His Majesties most gracious Message for Peace from Holdenby, *with His Answer to the Propositions.*

CHARLES R.

AS the daily expectation of the comming of the Propositions hath made His Majesty this long time to forbear giving His Answer unto them, so the appearance of their sending being no more for any thing He can hear, then it was at His first comming hither, notwithstanding that the Earl of *Louderdale* hath been at *London* above these ten daies, (whose not coming was said to be the onely stop) hath caused His Majesty thus to anticipate their coming to Him, and yet considering His Condition, that His Servants are denied accesse to Him, all but very few, and those by appointment, not His own Election, and that it is declared a crime for any but the Commissioners, or such who are particularly permitted by them, to converse with His Majesty, or that any Letters should be given to, or received from Him, may He not truly say, that He is not in case fit to make Concessions, or give Answers, since He is not master of those ordinary Actions which are the undoubted Rights of any free-born man, how mean soever his birth be? And certainly he would still be silent as to this subject, untill His Condition were much mended, did He not prefer such a right understanding betwixt Him and His Parliaments of both Kingdoms, which may make a firm and lasting Peace in all His Dominions, before any particular of His own, or any earthly blessing: and therefore His Majesty hath diligently imployed His utmost

indevours

indevours for divers moneths paft, fo to inform His Underftanding, and fatisfie His Confcience, that He might
be able to give fuch Anfwers to the Propofitions, as
would be moft agreeable to His Parliaments ; but He
ingenuoufly profeffes, that notwithftanding all the pains
that He hath taken therein, the nature of fome of them
appears fuch unto Him, that without difclaiming that
Reafon which God hath given him to judge by, for the
good of Him and His People, and without putting the
greateft violence upon His own Confcience, He cannot
give His confent to all of them. Yet His Majefty (that it
may appear to all the World how defirous He is to give
full fatisfaction) hath thought fit hereby to expreffe His
readineffe to grant what He may, and His willingneffe to
receive from them, and that perfonally if His two Houfes at *Weftminfter* fhall approve thereof, fuch further Information in the reft as may beft convince His judgment, and fatisfie thofe doubts which are not yet clear
unto Him, defiring them alfo to confider that if His Majefty intended to wind Himfelf out of thefe troubles by
indirect means, were it not eafie for Him now readily to
confent to what hath, or fhall be propofed unto Him ;
and afterwards chufe His time to break all, alleaging,
that forc'd Conceffions are not to be kept ? furely He
might, and not incur a hard cenfure from indifferent
men. But maximes in this kind are not the guides of
His Majefties actions, for He freely and clearly avows,
that He holds it unlawfull for any man, and moft bafe
in a King to recede from His promifes for having been
obtained by force or under reftraint ; wherefore His Majefty not only rejecting thofe acts which He efteems unworthy of Him, but even paffing by that which he might
well infift upon, a point of honour, in refpect of His pre-

sent condition, thus answers the first Proposition. That upon His Majesties coming to *London*, He will heartily joyne in all that shall concern the Honour of His two Kingdomes or the Assembly of the States of *Scotland*, or of the Commissioners or Deputies of either Kingdome, particularly in those things which are desired in that Proposition, upon confidence that all of them respectively with the same tendernes will look upon those things which concern His Majesties Honour.

In answer to all the Propositions concerning Religion, His Majesty proposeth, that He will confirm the Presbyteriall Government, the Assembly of Divines at *Westminster*, and the Directory, for three years, being the time set down by the two Houses, so that His Majesty and His Houshold be not hindred from that form of Gods Service which they formerly have; And also, that a free consultation and debate be had with the Divines at *Westminster* (twenty of His Majesties nomination being added unto them) whereby it may be determined by His Majesty and the two Houses how the Church shall be governed after the said three years or sooner, if differences may be agreed. Touching the Covenant, His Majesty is not yet therein satisfied, & desires to respite His particular answer thereunto until His coming to *London*, because it being a matter of conscience He cannot give a resolution therein till He may be assisted with the advice of some of His own Chaplains (which hath hitherto been denied Him) and such other Divines as shal be most proper to inform Him therein; and then He will make clearly appear, both His zeal to the Protestant profession, and the Union of these two Kingdoms, which He conceives to be the main drift of this Covenant. To the seventh and eighth Propositions, His Majesty will consent.

fent. To the ninth, His Majesty doubts not but to give
good satisfaction when He shall be particularly informed
how the said penalties shall be levied and disposed of.
To the tenth, His Majesties answer is, That He hath been
alwaies ready to prevent the practices of Papists, and
therefore is content to passe an Act of Parliament for
that purpose; And also, that the Laws against them be
duly executed. His Majesty will give His consent to the
Act for the due observation of the Lords Day, for the
suppressing of Innovations, and those concerning the
Preaching of Gods Word, and touching Non-Resi-
dence and Pluralities, and His Majesty will yeild to such
Act or Acts as shall be requisite to raise monies for the
payment and satisfying all publike Debts, expecting also
that his will be therein included. As to the Proposition
touching the *Militia*, though his Majesty cannot confent unto it *in terminis* as it is proposed, because thereby
he conceives, he wholly parts with the power of the
Sword entrusted to him by God and the Laws of the
Land, for the protection and government of his people,
thereby at once devesting himself, and dif-inheriting his
Posterity of that right and prerogative of the Crowne,
which is absolutely necessary to the Kingly Office, and
so weaken Monarchy in this Kingdom, that little more
then the name and shadow of it will remain : yet if it
be only security for the preservation of the Peace of this
Kingdom, after the unhappy troubles, and the due performance of all the agreements which are now to be concluded, which is desired, (which his Majesty alwaies understood to be the case, and hopes that herein he is not
miftaken)his Majesty will give aboundant satisfaction, to
which end he is willing by Act of Parliament, That the
whole power of the *Militia*, both by Sea and Land for

the

the space of ten years be in the hands of such persons as the two Houses shall nominate, giving them power during the said term to change the said persons, and substitute others in their places at pleasure, and afterwards to return to the proper chanell again, as it was in the times of Queen *Elizabeth* and King *James* of blessed memory. And now His Majesty conjures His two Houses of Parliament, as they are Englishmen and lovers of Peace, by the duty they owe to His Majesty their King, and by the bowels of compassion they have to their fellow Subjects, that they wil accept of this his Majesties offer, wherby the joyfull news of Peace may be restored to this languishing Kingdom. His Majesty will grant the like to the Kingdome of *Scotland* if it be desired, and agree to all things that are propounded touching the conserving of peace betwixt the two Kingdoms.

Touching *Ireland* (other things being agreed) His Majesty will give satisfaction therein. As to the mutuall Declarations proposed to be established in both Kingdoms by Act of Parliament, And the Modifications, Qualifications, and Branches which follow in the Propositions, His Majesty only professes, that He doth not sufficiently understand, nor is able to reconcile many things contained in them; but this He well knoweth; That a generall Act of Oblivion is the best Bond of Peace; and that after intestine Troubles, the wisdom of this and other Kingdoms hath usually and happily in all ages granted generall Pardons, whereby the numerous discontentments of many Persons and Families otherwise exposed to ruine, might not become fewell to new disorders, or seeds to future troubles. His Majesty therefore desires, that His two Houses of Parliament would seriously descend into these considerations, and
likewise

likewiſe tenderly look upon His Condition herein, and
the perpetuall diſhonour that muſt cleave to Him, if He
ſhal thus abandon ſo many perſons of Condition & For-
tune that have ingaged themſelves with and for Him, out
of a ſenſe of Duty, & propounds as a very acceptable teſtimony of their affection to Him, That a generall Act of
Oblivion and free Pardon be forthwith paſſed by Act of
Parliament. Touching the new great Seal, His Majeſty is
very willing to confirm both it, and all the Acts done by
vertue thereof, untill this preſent time, ſo that it be not
thereby preſſed to make void thoſe Acts of His done by
vertue of His great Seal, which in honour and juſtice He
is obliged to maintain ; And that the future Government
therof may be in his Majeſty, according to the due courſe
of Law. Concerning the Officers mentioned in the 19.
Article, His Majeſty when he ſhall come to *Weſtminſter*
wil gratifie his Parliament all that poſſibly he may, without deſtroying the alterations which are neceſſary for the
Crown. His Majeſty wil willingly conſent to the Act for
the confirmation of the Priviledges and Cuſtomes of the
City of *London*, and all that is mentioned in the Propoſitions for their particular advantage. And now that His
Majeſty hath thus far indeavoured to comply with the
deſires of His two Houſes of Parliament, to the end that
this agreement may be firme and laſting, without the
leaſt face or queſtion of reſtraint to blemiſh the ſame,
His Majeſty earneſtly deſires preſently to be admitted to
His Parliment at *Weſtminſter*, with that Honour which
is due to their Soveraign, there ſolemnly to confirm the
ſame, and legally to paſſe the Acts before mentioned, and
to give and receive as well ſatisfaction in all the remaining particulars, as likewiſe ſuch other pledges of mutuall
love, truſt, and confidence as ſhall moſt concern the

K 3   good

good of him, and his people ; upon which happy agreement, his Majesty will dispatch his Directions to the
Prince his Son, to return immediately to him, and will
undertake for his ready obedience thereunto.

Holdenby, May 12. 1647.

For the Speaker of the House of Peers pro tempore,
*To be Communicated to the two Houses of Parlia-
ment at* Westminster, *and the Commissioners of
the Parliament of* Scotland.

WHen our *Saviour* was *tempted in the wildernesse,* He was
(as Saint *Marke* saies) *among the wild beasts* there ; so
was our *Soveraigne* (as it seems) at *Holdenby :* but these were
worse mannered to the King, then those other were to Christ,
and lesse civill a great deal ; for these were *men* degenerated into *Beasts,* which of all others are the most savage ; we see in the
beginning of this Message, with what *barbarity,* and *inhumanity*
they behaved themselves towards Him, their Lord and Master,
who by Gods appointment had the just right and Dominion o-
ver them : they kept *His Servants from having accesse unto Him,*
not suffering one of His *owne Election* to come neer Him : they
declared it a crime for any of mankind *to converse or speak with
Him,* to *give any Letters to Him, or to receive any from Him :* no
commerce must He have with any Creature, but only such as were
His tormenters, and tempters, subservient to them, or allowed by
them : in brief, they would not let Him be *Master of those ordinary Actions, which belonged to any free-born man, of how mean a
birth soever :* insomuch that His Majesty may surely say, *He had to
do with Beasts at* Holdenby *in the shape of men, and fought with
them, as Saint* Paul *did at* Ephesus.

But (behold) for all this, though they forgot themselves to be
Subjects, and (indeed) *men,* yet He remembers Himself still to be
the Father of His People ; and though His Condition under them
might make Him *silent,* and His usage by them, might harden His
heart against them, and stir His spirit to plot revenge upon them ;
and

and to this end, to study *the winding Himself out of His Troubles by indirect means*; and that were (as Himself tells them) *by consenting readily, to what had, or should be proposed unto Him, and chuse a time afterward to break all, and alleage that forced Concessions are not to be kept, which* (he is confident) *He might do without incurring any hard censure from indifferent men.*

But His Majesties spirit is too *Kingly* and *divine*, to practice according to such *maximes* :. for though (indeed) no compulsions or violence shall be able to wrest from Him any Concessions againft Confcience, or in clear reafon againft the good and welfare of His people ; yet *He avows freely and cleerly that He holds it not only unlawfull, but base, to recede from His promises* (if once passed) *for having been obtained by force, or under restraint : wherefore His Majesty not only rejects all those Acts which He esteems unworthy of Him, but even passeth by that point of Honour, which He might well insist upon, in respect of His present Condition*, and confents as we fee fo far to all their Propofitions, as in Confcience and Reafon He conceived might poffibly be done, in order to His peoples welfare, though to the great diminution of His own undoubted *prerogative*, and moft *just rights* : for example, He knows well and acknowledgeth *(as we see) the power of the Sword is intrusted to Him by God and the Law, to Protect and Govern His people*, and is abfolutely neceffary to the *Kingly Office*, yet to *secure the Kingdome of peace* on His behalf, and *the performance of agreements* on His part, (which by reafon of the wrongs done Him was fo much fufpected,) He not only offers *the whole power of the Militia both by Sea and Land to be in the whole disposall of the two Houses of Parliament for ten years space*, but- alfo intreats them (after all this their ill ufage of Him) and conjures them, *as Englifh-men, and lovers of Peace, by the duty they owe Him, as their King, and by the Bowels of Compassion which they have to their fellow-Subjects, to accept of this His offer, whereby the joyfull news of Peace may be restored* (at length) *to this languishing Kingdom.*

Nay, and further (as we fee in this Meffage) notwithftanding they had grieved His fpirit by their unparalleld abufes, *and offended Him above seventy-times seven times*, and never hitherto fo much as faid, *it repenteth us* ; yet doth His moft gracious Majefty even urge upon them; (for the prevention of new diforders, and future

future troubles) to accept of *a pardon* at His Hand for all the
wrongs which they had done Him, and to admit of an *Act of oblivion,* as the *best bond of peace :* only He would have them deny
their Corruptions so far, as to cease thirsting for the bloud and
totall ruine of those of their Christian Brethren (whom they had
well nigh undone already) for their love and adherence to Himself, according to *their duties,* as Gods Word, the Law, their
Consciences, Oaths of Allegeance and Protestation did command
them : He desires (in effect) that their spleens may rest satisfied
with the wrongs already offered to these persons, and their families, lest their *discontent might haply prove fewell to new disorders :* He would have the *Act of Oblivion* to include them too :
Yea, He would have these men *(*who indeed only need it*)* to
consent that it might reach to all the people of the Land in generall ; *(*this is all He desires of them,*)* that so from henceforth we
might live together like Christians ; and not like Heathens, like
savage Creatures, or rather like devils any longer, as (alas) we
have done *(* to the unspeakable disgrace of the Gospell and
of our Nation) since these men domineered : And to the end,
that there might not be *the least face or question of His Majesties restraint to blemish this agreement* to their disadvantage in
after-times, *He earnestly desires* that Himself might *presently be
admitted to His two Houses ;* (after all this, His complyance) *to
perfect the same :*

And now surely, we must needs conclude that here was enough
to still the Clamour of these *men* against their King *(*had they not
been far worse then *beasts*) & to have conquered their spirits even
to everlasting : But they were resolute in their way, all this was
nothing in their esteem ; for indeed the established and *fundamen-
tall Laws* of the Land, are so severe against such as go in those
waies and courses which these have travailed so far in, against the
King and their fellow-subjects ; that they dare not trust either to
his *mercy,* or their *forgivenesse,* be the same never so strongly confirmed unto them ; nor can any *Act of Oblivion* in their con-
ceits) be ever able to obliterate the same : and therefore as if He
had offered nothing at all, they still cry out, that His Majesty *is
averse to Peace, and never yet pleased to accept of any Tender fit for
them to make, nor to offer any fit for them to receive :* and thei
                                                            Preacher

Preachers are still set awork by them to pray before the people, *that God would incline the Kings heart to come unto His Parliament.*

But these men not knowing how to answer His Majesty (saving their own stubborn resolutions,) or to say any thing to these His so large and gracious *tenders*, they even suffer Him after their old wont, to wait, and to live in expectation.

And yet we found (or at least supposed at that time) that His Majesties Answer to some of these Propositions, *viz.*to those that concerned *Religion* or *Church Goverment*, had some effect upon the *Independent party*, whose boyling discontents about this time began to vapour forth more furiously then before, against their *Presbyterian* Brethren ; whose *Government* and *Directory* His Majesty had here promised to confirm for three years, (the time set down by the two Houses) so that Himself and His, might not be hindered thereby in serving God the old and true way ; now upon this, the *untamed Heighfers* of this other faction, altogether unaccustomed to the yoak ; having observed that their *Brethrens little finger* was like to prove heavier *then the Bishops loynes :* were horribly loath to come under the fence of their *Scorpions*, and therefore began to cast about for themselves, and to devise a prevention of this *three years confirmation*, left they should feel the lash so long, and be kept under worse then an *Ægyptian* Bondage : and in order to this, they began to find fault (as there was cause) at the *Presbyterians* ill usage of the King, (for they indeed were His chief Tormenters at *Holdenby ;* Master *Marshall* and *his fellow-Minister* being then also of that faction, because at that time it was the most prevailing) they exclaimed on them for handling His Majesty so hardly, in keeping Him as a *Prisoner*, denying Him the freedome of His *Conscience*, and service of His *Chaplains :* they remembred also with much regret of spirit (as then seemed) the wicked tenents of *Buchanan*, *Knox*, and others, the erectors and propugnators of the *Presbyterian* Discipline in *Scotland*, about excommunicating, deposing, arraigning, and killing Princes : and their practices against *James* his Grand-mother, his Mother, and himself in his Infancy ; and they did plainly observe (as themselves said) by the carriages of these *Presbyterians* towards His Majesty at this present, that they resolved to tread in the same steps, as their predecessours had done before, notwith-

L   standing

standing their so many solemn *professions* and *protestations* to the Contrary : And hereupon they said *they thought it their duty* (according to their first ingagement in this war) *to bring the King to His Parliament* with *Safety* and *Honour*, that He might injoy the just rights of His *Crown*, as well as of His *Conscience* ; largely promising and protesting to be instruments of the same, to the content of His Majesty and the whole Kingdome ; and upon these pretences the King was delivered by them from that particular thraldome at *Holdenby* : And afterward brought with the applause and joy of His people, to His Manour of *Hampton*, where His Servants, and Chaplains at first were allowed accesse to Him, and many of His Subjects permitted to glad their hearts with the sight of Him. And this gleame of prosperity blazed well till the *Houses* were thinned of the chief Heads of the *contrary faction :* for in very deed all this was done to another end then was pretended, and ordered by other Councels then yet appeared ; it being the nature of some men to envy that any should be more injurious then themselves, or have a greater hand in acting evill then they. There were in the *Houses* (and elswhere) some *Grandees*, (as they are since called) that were ambitious of ingrossing the sole power over King and Kingdom, which others as yet had as large a share in managing of (if not a larger) then themselves, to exclude whom they made use of the *Independent* humour in the inferiour Officers and Souldiers, layed the plot for them, in that manner as it was acted, secretly provoked them to the undertaking, and countenanced them in it, when it was done, by pretending to be of their Religion ; clouding their maine *Designe*, all the while from the body of the Army ; whom they set a work to make certaine *Proposals*, partly in their owne behalf, and partly tending to those things which had been promised to the King ; while themselves in the *interim*, were dressing, or making ready to act the very same part, which *those* they disliked had done before ; and had been thus intermitted for a season, till *those others* were ejected or cast over-board : for the very same *Propositions* in Effect, that had formerly assaulted His Majesty at *Newcastle*, and were answered by Him from *Holdenby* (as we have seen) are (to renew His trouble) remitted to Him : which His Majesty returns Answer unto, in these words,

His Majesties seventeenth Message.

*His Majesties most gracious Answer to the Propositions,
presented to Him at* Hampton-Court.

CHARLS R.

HIs Majesty cannot chuse but be paſſionately ſenſible (as He believes all His good Subjects are).
of the late great diſtractions, and ſtill languiſh-
ing and unſetled ſtate of this Kingdome ; and He calls
God to witneſſe, and is willing to give teſtimony to all
the world of His readineſſe to contribute His utmoſt endevours for reſtoring it to a happy and flouriſhing condition. His Majesty having peruſed the Propoſitions
now brought to Him, finds them the ſame in effect,
which were offered to Him at *Newcaſtle.* To ſome of
which as He could not then conſent without violation of
His Conſcience and Honour ; So neither can He agree to
others, now conceiving them in many reſpects more diſ-
agreeable to the preſent condition of affairs, then when
they were formerly preſented unto Him, as being deſtructive to the main principall Intereſts of the Army, and
of all thoſe, whoſe Affections concur with them. And
His Majesty having ſeen the Propoſals of the Army to
the Commiſſioners from His two Houſes reſiding with
them, and with them to be treated on, in order to the
clearing and ſecuring of the Rights and Liberties of the
Kingdome, and the ſetling of a juſt and laſting Peace.
To which Propoſals, as He conceives His two Houſes
not to be ſtrangers ; So He believes they will think with
Him, that they much more conduce to the ſatisfaction
of all Intereſts, and may be a fitter foundation for a laſting Peace, then the Propoſitions which at this time are
tendred unto Him. He therefore propounds (as the beſt

way

way in His judgment in order to a Peace) That His two Houses would inftantly take into confideration thofe Propofals, upon which there may be a Perfonall Treaty with His Majefty, and upon fuch other Propofitions as his Majefty fhal make: hoping that the faid Propofitions may be fo moderated in the faid Treaty, as to render them the more capable of his Majefties full conceffion: Wherein He refolves to give full fatisfaction to His people, for whatfoever fhall concern the fetling of the Proteftant Profeffion, with liberty to tender Confcien-ces, and the fecuring of the Laws, Liberties and Proper-ties of all His Subjects, and the juft Priviledges of Par-liaments for the future: and likewife by His prefent de-portment in this Treaty, He will make the world clearly judge of his intentions in matters of future Government. In which Treaty His Majefty will be well pleafed (if it be thought fit) that Commiffioners from the Army, (whofe the Propofals are) may likewife be admitted. His Majefty therefore conjures his two Houfes of Parlia-ment, by the duty they owe to God, and his Majefty their King, and by the bowels of compaffion they have to their fellow-fubjects, both for the relief of their pre-fent fufferings, & to prevent future miferies, that they will forthwith accept of this his Majefties Offer, whereby the joyfull newes of Peace may be reftored to this diftreffed Kingdome; And for what concerns the Kingdome of *Scotland* mentioned in the Propofitions, his Majefty will very willingly Treat upon thofe particulars with the Scotch Commiffioners; and doubts not, but to give rea-fonable fatisfaction to that his Kingdome.

At Hampton-court *the 9. of Septemb.* 1647.

> *For the Speaker of the Houfe of Peers*
> pro tempore, *to be communicated,* &c.

It appeares by this Meffage of His Majeftie, and more fully by the *Propofitions* themfelves, which it relates unto, that the *Tragedie* is ftill the fame, the variation is onely of the *Actors*, not of the *Scene :* Nor did thofe *Pharifees* defire his death and down-fall more, then thefe *Suduces* doe, and will endeavour to prevent His Refurrection. Tis the fame *Leven* that *fowres* both factions, and the controverfie between them only is, which fhall be the chief, or have moft ftrength to expreffe moft *fowreneffe.*

But His Majefty finds a difference in the prefent condition of Affairs, from what they were at the former prefentment of thefe *Propofitions ;* for they feemed to be totally deftructive to the *interefts of the Army*, (now more manifeft to Him then before) whom His Majefty was pleafed to look on (at this prefent) not only as *Subjects*, but as *Friends ;* and being defirous in His Princely care and equity (as a common Father) to give fatisfaction to all His people, doth (as we fee) in His *wifdome* and *publick affections* anfwer accordingly ; and fince the *Army* had been *their Servants* and *Hirelings* (though againft Himfelf their naturall Leige Lord) yet He thinks it meet in His *Fatherly Clemency* not only to paffe by what they had done, (as acts of *ignorance* in them) but alfo to endeavour that they be payed their wages ; and to this end commends their cafe and *Propofalls*, to thofe their Mafters who had imployed them, and fent thefe *Propofitions* unto Him : And that all parties may have content, He defires againe a *Perfonall Treaty* with them for *Peace*, whereunto He is well pleafed (for His part) *if it be thought fit* (as he fayes) *that Commiffioners from the Army may alfo be admitted ;* that fo without more adoe, a cleare, open, and full fatisfaction might be given to all parties : And fure the Soldiers, as well as the reft of his abufed, and deluded people, will find in the end , that the King will prove their beft friend and pay-mafter ; who in the meane time (as they may obferve) makes Himfelfe even a Petitioner in their behalfe, to His two Houfes ; whom He conjures againe (as He had done oft before) *by the duty they owe to God, to Himfelfe their King, and by the bowels of compaffion which they have* (or ought to have) *to their fellow-fubjects ;* to give way, that their prefent fufferings may be relieved, their future miferies prevented , and *the joyfull newes of Peace againe reftored.*

L. 3 But

But this request and conjuration of His Majesty at the present, found no other respect with the new *purged Houses*, then His other before had done, when (by their owne confessions) these Houses were so *filthy* and *uncleane* : indeed the *purging* was not compleatly done, according to the *Law of clensing*, for the *Leprosie* that hath so troubled us all, was (as now appeares) spread to the *very walls*, and *stones*, and *morter* it self, all which should have been taken away, and other *stones* and *morter* put in the place thereof, that is, *New Houses* should have been throughly framed of new materials, and so the *Plague* might have been quite healed, which upon this default grew worse ere long, then it had been before, as if the *evill spirit* had been onely thrust out, to *fetch in seven more spirits worse, and more wicked then himselfe :* for not long after His Majesty had sent this last Message or Answer, He was forced back to His former Condition of Captivity, He is circled with Armies, watched by Soldiers, yea hath strict and strange guards set and doubled upon Him, and His servants that were formerly admitted, excluded from Him. In a word, He is reduced to the same (if not to a worse) condition by his *Deliverers* at *Hampton Court*, then that was which they pretended to free him from at *Holdenby*. For some amongst them whisperingly threatned also his sudden destruction, and to act the Assassinates part upon His Sacred Person : Whereupon for the safety of His life, He was forced to retire speedily, and privately from that place & in the night season, when the weather was wet, cold, stormy tempestuous ; at which time He left this insuing *Declaration* behinde Him on the *Table*, which speaks aboundantly, His great wisdome, and strong affections towards the Peace and Happinesse of all His People, not excepting His very Enemies, notwithstanding His Barbarous and Hard usage at their Hands.

His *Majesties* eighteenth *Message*.

His Majesties most Gracious Declaration, left by Him on
His Table at Hampton Court, Novemb. 11. 1647.

CHARLS R.

LIberty being that which in all times hath been, but
especially now is the common theame and desire
of all men ; common Reason shews, that Kings
lesse then any should endure captivity: And yet, I call
God and the world to witnesse, with what patience I
have endured a tedious restraint : which so long as I had
any hopes that this sort of my suffering might conduce
to the peace of my Kingdoms, or the hindring of more
effusion of bloud, I did willingly undergoe : but now
finding by too certain proofs, that this my continued
patience would not onely turn to my personall ruine, but
likewise be of much more prejudice, then furtherance to
the publique good ; I thought I was bound as well by
Naturall, as Politicall obligations, to seek my safety, by
retiring my self for some time, from the publick view
both of my friends and enemies : And I appeal to all
indifferent men, to judge, if I have not just cause to free
my selfe from the hands of those, who change their Principles with their condition ; and who are not ashamed
openly to intend the destruction of the Nobility, taking
away their Negative Voice ; and with whom, the Level-
lers doctrine, is rather countenanced then punished :
And as for their intentions to my Person, their changing,
and putting more strict Guards upon me, with the dif-
charging most of all those Servants of mine, who formerly they willingly admitted to wait upon me, does
suffici-

sufficiently declare. Nor would I have this my retirement mif-interpreted ; for I shall earneftly and unceffant-
ly endeavour the fetling of a fafe and well-grounded
Peace, where ever I am or shall be ; and that (as much as
may be) without the effusion of more Chriftian blood :
for which how many times have I defired, preft to be
heard, and yet no ear given to me ? And can any reafonable man think, that (according to the ordinary courfe
of affaires) there *can be a fetled Peace without it ? Or that
God will bleffe thofe, who refufe to hear their own King ?
Surely no. Nay I muft farther adde, that (befides what con-
cernes my felfe) unleffe all other chief interefts, have not
onely a hearing, but likewife juft fatisfaction given unto
them, (to wit, the Presbyterians, Independents, Army, thofe
who have adhered to me, and even the Scots) I fay there cannot (I speak not of Miracles, it being in my opinion, a fin-
full prefumption, in fuch cafes, to expect or truft to them)
be a fafe or lafting Peace.*

Now as I cannot deny, but that my perfonall fecurity
is the urgent caufe of this my retirement ; fo I take God
to witneffe, that the publike Peace is no leffe before my
eyes : and I can finde no better way to expreffe this my
profeffion (I know not what a wifer may doe) then by
defiring and urging that all chief Interefts may be heard,
to the end each may have juft fatisfaction : As for
example, the Army, (for the reft , though neceffary,
yet I fuppofe are not difficult to content) ought (in
my judgment) to enjoy the liberty of their confciences,
have an Act of Oblivion or Indempnity (which fhould
extend to all the reft of my Subjects) and that all their
Arrears fhould be fpeedily and duly paid ; which I will
undertake to doe, fo I may be heard, and that I be not
hindred from ufing fuch lawfull and honeft means as I
                                                    fhall

shall chuse. To conclude, let me be heard with Free-dome, Honour and Safety, and I shall instantly breake through this Cloud of Retirement, and shew my selfe really to be *Pater Patriæ*.

Hampton-Court, Novemb. 11. 1647.

> *For the Speaker of the House of Peers* pro tempore,
> *To be Communicated to the two Houses of Parlia-*
> *ment at* Westminster, *and the Commissioners of*
> *the Parliament of* Scotland.

HE that reads His Majesty in these His Messages and Decla-rations, and considers well the discovery made therein of His disposition, must needs conclude, that *never King since Chrifts time, was indued with more of Chrifts spirit.*

In this Declaration we observe among many other things wor-thy our speciall notice, three particulars.

1. His Majesties most *Christian and fatherly Affection* to us all in generall, How like a truly good Shepherd He did *willingly un-dergo and indure a most tedious restraint,* so long as He had hopes that the same might *conduce* any thing *to our peace,* and prevent the further *effusion of our Blood :* but when He saw by certaine proofs, that His continued patience was likely to turn onely to His Personall ruine, whereby ours, and that of the publike would certainly be hastened : He thought Himself bound to endevour His peoples safety by His own, *in retiring for some time from pub-like view.*

2. His Majesties *great care* of preserving the being of the *Eng-lish Nobility* whose *destruction* he perceived was *openly intended,* as well as His ; by those that aymed at *the taking away their Nega-tive voice.* Had those of them, who have so shamefully degene-rated with the times from the dignity of their Aunceftors, been as carefull of His *Honour* and *Rights,* as He (we see) is and hath been of theirs : both He, and they, and we all, had not been so miserable at this present ; when God shall lay this sin unto their Charge, *woe, woe, woe,* will be unto them.

M　　　　　　　　3. His

3. His Majesties *fervent desire* that *all Interests may be Heard,* and juſt ſatisfaction given to them ; the *Presbyterians, Independants, Army, Scots* and all, who have combined together and ingaged againſt Him, as wel as thoſe who had adhered to Him ; and yet none of them (except thoſe) had evidenced any full readineſſe of mind that He might be reſtored to thoſe *His rights* which God and the Law commands ſhould be given to Him.

Concerning Himſelf, we obſerve He desires but only to be Heard, and that for theſe two Ends : firſt to procure peace for His people, which is not probably otherwiſe to be ſetled ; and Secondly, to prevent Gods Curſe from falling upon His Gain-ſayers which otherwiſe is moſt likely to overwhelme them : His words (we ſee) are theſe, *Can any reasonable man think that (according to the ordinary course of affairs) there can be a setled peace without it ? or that God will blesse those who refuse to hear their own King? Surely no.* May His Majeſty obtain but hopes of this, He will *instantly break through His cloud of Retirement, and shew Himself really to be,* (as indeed He hath alwaies been) *Pater patriæ.*

But can His Majeſty conceal His *Affection* ſo long ? can He forbear ſoliciting His peoples peace till Himſelf be *Heard* ? 'tis impoſſible, no, no, He cannot contain Himſelf ſeven daies from returning to His former labour in vain, *or fruitlesse endevours* ; but ſets immediately to the ſame again ſo ſoon as He arrived at the *Iſle of Wight,* the place of His retirement, though whether deſtined ſo to be, by His own choice, or others deſignation, time will diſcover : But it plainly appears, His Majeſty had a good opinion of the *Army in Generall,* in His not removing quite from among them, and of the *Governour* of that place in particular, or elſe being in a free or open road, and in the night ſeaſon, He might eaſily have turned ſome other way : He removed from *Hampton-Court, Novemb.* the 11. and on the 17. of the ſame Month, He writes from *Wight* this which follows.

His *Majesties nineteenth Message.*

His Majesties most Gracious Message from the Isle *of* Wight : *for a Personall Treaty for Peace.*

CHARLES R.

His Majesty is confident that before this time, His two Houses of Parliament have received the Message which He left behind Him at *Hampton-Court* the eleventh of this Month, by which they will have understood the reasons which enforced Him to go from thence, as likewise His constant endeavours, for the setling of a safe and wel-grounded Peace wheresoever He should be ; And being now in a place, where He conceives Himself to be at much more freedome and security then formerly ; He thinks it necessary (not only for making good of His own professions, but also for the speedy procuring of a Peace in these languishing and distressed Kingdoms) at this time to offer such grounds to His two Houses for that effect ; which upon due examination of all Interests, may best conduce thereunto.

And because Religion is the best and chiefest foundation of Peace, His Majesty will begin with that Particular.

That for the abolishing Arch-bishops, Bishops, &c. His Majesty cleerly professeth, that He cannot give His consent thereunto, both in relation as He is a Christian, and a King : For the first, He avows that He is satisfied in His Judgement, that this order was placed in the Church by the Apostles themselves ; and ever since their time, hath continued in all Christian Churches through-

M 2   out

out the world, untill this laft century of years; And in this Church in all times of Change and Reformation, it hath beén upheld by the wifdome of His Anceftours, as the great preferver of Doctrine, Difcipline, and Order in the fervice of God. As a King at His Coronation, He hath not only taken a Solemn Oath, to maintain this Order, but His Majefty and His Predeceffours in their confirmations of the Great Charter, have infeperably woven the right of the Church into the Liberties of the reft of the Subjects: And yet He is willing, it be provided that the particular Bifhops perform the feverall Duties of their callings, both by their perfonall refidence and frequent Preachings in their Dioceffes, as alfo that they exercife no act of Jurifdiction or Ordination, without the confent of their Presbyters; And will confent, that their Powers in all things be fo limited, that they be not grievous to tender Confciences: Wherefore, fince His Majefty is willing to give eafe to the Confciences of others, He fees no reafon why He alone, and thofe of His Judgment, fhould be Preffed to a violation of theirs. Nor can His Majefty confent to the Alienation of Church Lands, becaufe it cannot be denied to be a fin of the higheft Sacriledge; as alfo, that it fubverts the intentions of fo many pious Donors, who have laid a heavy curfe upon all fuch profane violations, which His Majefty is very unwilling to undergoe; And befides the matter of Confcience, His Majefty believes it to be a prejudice to the Publike good, many of His Subjects having the benefit of renuing Leafes at much eafier Rates, then if thofe poffeffions were in the hands of private men; not omitting the difcouragement which it will be to all learning and induftry, when fuch eminent rewards fhal be taken away,

which

which now lie open to the Children of meaneſt Perſons.

Yet His Majeſty conſidering the great preſent diſtempers concerning Church Diſcipline, and that the Presbyterian Government is now in practice, His Majeſty to eſchew confuſion as much as may be, and for the ſatisfaction of His two Houſes, is content that the ſaid Government be legally permitted to ſtand, in the ſame condition it now is for three years; Provided, that His Majeſty and thoſe of His Judgment (or any other who cannot in Conſcience ſubmit thereunto) be not obliged to comply with the Presbyter.all Government, but have free practice of their own Profeſſion, without receiving any prejudice thereby; and that a free conſultation and debate be had with the Divines at *Weſtminſter* (twenty of His Majeſties nomination being added unto them) whereby it may be determined by His Majeſty and the two Houſes, how the Church Government after the ſaid time ſhall be ſetled, (or ſooner if differences may be agreed) as is moſt agreeable to the Word of God; with full liberty to all thoſe who ſhall differ upon conſciencious grounds from that ſetlement; alwaies provided, that nothing aforeſaid be underſtood to tolerate thoſe of the Popiſh Profeſſion, nor the exempting of any Popiſh Recuſant from the penalties of the Laws, or to tolerate the publiké profeſſion of Atheiſme or Blaſpemy, contrary to the doctrine of the Apoſtles, Nicene and Athanaſian Creeds, they having been received by, and had in reverence of all the Chriſtian Churches, and more particularly by this of *England*, ever ſince the Reformation.

Next, the *Militia* being that right, which is inſeparably and undoubtedly inherent in the Crown, by the Laws of this Nation, and that which former Parliaments,

M 3

ments, as likewise·this, hath acknowledged fo to be ;
His Majefty cannot fo much wrong that truft which the
Laws of God and this Land hath annexed to the Crown
for the protection and fecurity of his People, as to diveft
Himfelf and Succeffours of the power of the Sword : yet
to give an infallible evidence of His defire to fecure the
performance of fuch agreements as fhall be made in order to a Peace, his Majefty wil confent to an Act of Parliament, that the whole power of the *Militia* both by Sea
and Land, for and during his whole Reign, fhall be ordered and difpofed by his two Houfes of Parliament, or
by fuch perfons as they fhall appoint, with powers limited for fuppreffing of Forces within· this Kingdom, to
the difturbance of the publike Peace, and againft for-
raigne Invafion ; and that they fhall have power during
his faid Reigne, to raife Monies for the purpofes aforefaid ; and that neither his Majefty that now is, or any o-
ther (by any authority derived only from him) fhall exe-
cute any of the faid Powers during his Majefties faid
Reigne, but fuch as fhall act by the confent and approbation of the two Houfes of Parliament : Neverthelefse
his Majefty intends that all Patents, Commiffions, and
other Acts concerning the *Militia*, be made and acted as
formerly ; and that after his Majefties Reign, all the
power of the *Militia* fhall return entirely to the Crown,
as it was in the times of *Q. Elizabeth,* and *K. James* of
blefsed memory.

    After this head of the *Militia*, the confideration of the
Arrears due to the Army is not improper to follow ; for
the payment whereof, and the eafe of his People, his Majefty is willing to concur in any thing that can be done
without the violation of his Confcience and Honour.
Wherefore if his two Houfes fhall confent to remit unto
him

him ſuch benefit out of Sequeſtations from *Michaelmas* laſt, and out of Compoſitions that ſhall be made before the concluding of the peace, and the Arrears of ſuch as have been already made, the aſſiſtance of the Clergy, and the Arrears of ſuch Rents of his own Revenue as his two Houſes ſhall not have received before the concluding of the Peace, his Majeſty will undertake within the ſpace of eighteen Months, the payment of four hundred thouſand pounds for the ſatisfaction of the Army : And if thoſe means ſhall not be ſufficient, his Majeſty intends to give way to the ſale of Forreſt Lands for that purpoſe, this being the Publike Debt which in his Majeſties judgment is firſt to be ſatisfied ; and for other publike debts already contracted upon Church Lands or any other Ingagements, his Majeſty will give his conſent to ſuch Act or Acts for raiſing of Monies for payment thereof as both Houſes ſhall hereafter agree upon, ſo as they be equally laid, whereby his people (already too heavily burthened by theſe late diſtempers) may have no more preſſures upon them then this abſolute neceſſity requires : And for the further ſecuring of all fears, his Majeſty will conſent, that an Act of Parliament be paſſed for the diſpoſing of the great Offices of State, and naming of Privy Counſellours for the whole terme of his Raigne by the two Houſes of Parliament, their Patents and Commiſſions being taken from his Majeſty, and after to return to the Crown, as is expreſt in the Article of the *Militia.* For the Court of Wards and Liveries, his Majeſty very well knows the conſequence of taking that away, by turning of all Tenures into common Soccage, as well in point of Revenue to the Crown, as in the Protection of many of his Subjects being Infants. Neverthelèſſe if the continuance thereof ſeem

grievous

grievous to His Subjects, rather then he will fail on His part in giving satisfaction, He will consent to an Act for taking of it away, so as a full recompence be setled upon His Majesty and his Successours in perpetuity, and that the Arrears now due be reserved unto Him towards the payment of the Arrears of the Army.

And that the memory of these late distractions may be wholly wiped away, His Majesty will consent to an Act of Parliament for the suppressing and making null of all Oaths, Declarations and Proclamations against both or either House of Parliament, and of all Indictments and other proceedings against any persons for adhering unto them; and His Majesty proposeth, (as the best expedient to take away all seeds of future differences) that there be an Act of Oblivion to extend to all His Subjects.

As for *Ireland*, the Cessation there is long since determined, but for the future (all other things being fully agreed) His Majesty will give full satisfaction to his Houses concerning that Kingdom.

And although His Majesty cannot consent in Honour and Justice to avoid all His own Grants and Acts past under His Great Seal since the 22 of *May*, 1642. or to the confirming of all the Acts and Grants passed under that made by the two Houses, yet His Majesty is confident, that upon perusall of particulars, He shall give full satisfaction to His two Houses, to what may be reasonably desired in that particular.

And now His Majesty conceives that by these His offers (which He is ready to make good upon the setlement of a Peace) He hath clearly manifested His intentions to give full security and satisfaction to all Interests, for what can justly be desired in order to the future happinesse of His people. And for the perfecting of these

Con-

Concessions, as also for such other things as may be proposed by the two Houses, and for such just and reasonable demands as his Majesty shal find necessary to propose on His part, He earnestly desires a Personall Treaty at *London* with His two Houses, in Honour, Freedom and Safety, it being in His judgment the most proper, and indeed, only means to a firm and setled Peace, and impossible without it to reconcile former, or avoid future misunderstandings.

All these things being by Treaty perfected, His Majesty believes His two Houses will think it reasonable, that the Proposals of the Army concerning the Succession of Parliaments and their due Elections, should be taken into consideration.

As for what concerns the Kingdom of *Scotland*, His Majesty will very readily apply Himself to give all reasonable satisfaction, when the desires of the two Houses of Parliament on their behalf, or of the Commissioners of that Kingdom, or of both joyned together, shall be made known unto Him.

CHARLS R.

From the Isle of Wight, *Novemb.* 17. 1647.

To the Speaker of the House of Peers pro tempore, *to be communicated to the two Houses of Parliament at* Westminster, *and to the Commissioners of the Parliament of* Scotland.

WE see at the beginning of this Message, that His Majesty *conceived Himself to be at much more freedome and security in that place, then formerly* : Had the Governour there been a true Gentleman in the least degree, he would rather have lost his life, then crossed His Majesties opinion in that particular : but we are

N confirmed

confirmed by Him, in what we knew before, that *swordmen in these dayes, are not all men of Honesty, nor yet of Honour.*

His Majesty being now in His own apprehension, *at more free-dome,* renews His motions for the purchase of *peace,* that his jealous and hardhearted Chapmen (if possible) might be cured of all their feares, in seeing now, that His profers before, were not the fruits of *restraint,* but of *Hearty will and Affections* to His languishing and distressed Kingdomes.

And first, His Majesty (in this Message) declares His Conscience and Reasons, why He cannot consent to the totall Alteration of that Church Government, which He had *sworn* to maintain; and they without any Conscience or Reasons at all would *force* Him to destroy: Doubtlesse if there were a necessity, that it must be as they would have it, yet would it better become them to endeavour His Majesties satisfaction in the matter, and to Answer His Reasons, then to urge him with violence to goe against both; & when they see He dares not for offending God, yet to bawl and clamour against Him without shame or Honesty, as if He made no Conscience at all of His Oath taken at His Coronation.

But what necessity is there of pulling up this *pale* of Government, save only to let *wild beasts* into Gods vineyard? surely if his Majesty were not confirmed in His Judgement, that this *pale* was of the Apostles *setting,* and cherished *in all Christian Churches,* since their times (*till this last Century of years*) and *upheld* in this particular Church since the *Reformation,* as the speciall *preserver of Doctrine and order in Gods Worship:* and if He had not *taken an Oath at His Coronation, to maintaine it;* and though *the rights of the Church were not so woven as they be in the great Charter of the Kingdome, with the Liberties of the rest of His Subjects;* yet as He is a King and protector of Christs Religion, as He is a nursing Father of His Church, beholding the present destruction and vastation of both, by those swarms of Hereticks and Schismaticks, which have abounded within these seven years, since the Execution of this Government hath been suspended; He ought in *Conscience* and *Prudence* to endeavour the continuance of it, it being by the confession of its greatest Adversaries, (*viz.* the *Smectymnists*) first established to suppresse and prevent these very mischiefs.

His

His Majesty will see that Bishops doe their duties, and that all abuses in the Government be amended, which no question but the Tryenniall Parliament will also look unto, (if the Kingdome might but be blessed with it.) And that the present Enemies of this Government may have both time and occasion to think better of their own demands in their cooler temper: His Majesty is willing to let them for their own parts to try three years how well they can thrive without it, hoping that their Mistris Experience, may have taught them by that time, in the *want* of this Government, the *necessity* of the use and continuation of it; but to consent to the *totall abolition* of that which to Himself and all sober men is evident to be the most speciall mean to preserve the life, being, and beauty of Chrifts Church, no men but these that drive Satans designe (if they well consider of it) can, or will desire it.

2. His Majesty plainly declares, that he dares not be a partaker in that Sinne of *the highest Sacriledge*, by consenting to the *Alienation of Church-lands*, nor venture upon the *Curses* which hang over the heads of such *profane violaters*, as those are and will be, that shall deal in such merchandize; for *His Majesty feared God*. Nor can He be induced so much to prejudice *the publick good*, or to damnifie so many of His Subjects, who farme these Lands (as now held) at far easier rates then they are like to doe, if they should become the possessions of private men; for *the King loves His People*. Nor lastly, will He ever be such an ill friend to learning and industry, as to consent to the taking away of those *rewards* which excite and courage thereunto the meanest persons; for *our Soveraign Lord Honours Learning* so much, that in relation to that, He will provide and keep maintenance in store for the Children of His lowest Subjects.

Nay, should His Majesty yeeld to this *Sacriledge*, were it not the next way to destroy Religion as well as Learning? *Julian the Apostate*, one of the greatest and subtillest enemies that ever *Christianity* had, thought it was: And therefore he endeavouring to extirpate the same, made *an Ordinance for the sale of Church lands*, or the taking away of *Clergie maintenance*; the renewment of which, might in prudence have been omitted by the pretenders to Christianity of these dayes, for *Julians* sake.

These be the two things which His Majesty denyes His consent unto,

unto, *Abolition of Church Government*, and *Alienation of Church Revennes*: and his Reasons for the same are far better, then any we know he can have, for his yeelding those things which he offers to them; whereof the first is the *power* of the *Militia both by sea and land, during his owne whole raigne*,which he is content shall be ordered and disposed of by *His two Houses, and such as they shall appoint*: And his Reason for this is, *to give an infallible evidence of His desire to secure the performance of such agreement as shall be made in order to Peace*: Whereby His Majesty seemes to us (to speak in their phrase) *even to yeeld up not onely His Will and Affections, but also His very Reason and Judgement, for the obtaining a good Accommodation.*

But concerning the reality of His Majesties Desires in this particular, the best of His people neither wish nor need any such evidence; the *security* is onely doubted and desired on their parts, whom we have seen and found so false and perfidious already both to the King,and the whole Kingdome: Nor (if it were possible, this proffer of His Maj.could secure us of them)dare we the Christian people of this Nation, (whose servants they are) give our consent, that the *Sword* should be out of that Hand where God hath put it for our good; for *Nolumus hos regnare*, we are resolved on that: we will never live under the tyrannie of these men: The Wise-man hath said it, and we have found it by wofull experience, *That by the raigne of servants, the earth is disquieted.*

But God hath been much our friend in this matter, in hardning their hearts against this *proffer*,which in pity to us his peeled and distressed people, to purchase peace for us, this our most compassionate and self-denying King was pleased to tender: and we are with fervour of spirit to praise the Majesty of heaven for it, it being an earnest, or ground of hope, that he hath yet some mercy in store for this poore Nation; that He will not suffer it to lie under so heavy a guilt, as the impunity of so much evill would be hazardous to bring upon it, by an Act of Oblivion. No,no,our God will have these mischievous vermine destroyed by the sword of Justice, (as we hope) and not of Judgement,and,so shall the curse of God which hangs over the Land for those many blasph mies against Majesty, those unlawfull oathes, those bloods and oppressions which have been committed in it by these men be removed from

from it, and then the fame fhall enjoy reft and peace againe, under the protection of her moft gracious and indulgent Soveraigne. And in the mean time we are to pray fervently, that this our good King may ftill afford us his true *affections*, and thefe onely, but may from henceforth keep his *Will*, his *Reafon* and *Judgement* folely to himfelfe, yea and his *power* too ; for we are well affured from our experience both of *Him* and *Them*, that He alone is able and ready to manage all to our benefit, a great deale better then any elfe either will or can : And God we hope will encline His Majefties heart to obferve his hand in this conftant temper of their fpirits hitherto againft all His gracious offers of this nature.

We obferve alfo in the next place, how His Majefty takes into confideration the Arreares of their Army , or the wants of thofe Soldiers which *they* the raifers of, were more carefull to *lift* then they are to *pay* : their fervants we know they were, raifed and imployed by them againft Him, and now kept together in a needy & bare condition to burden His people, and to keep them in continuall feare, poverty, and bondage : even this very Army, for their fatisfaction, and His peoples eafe, His Majefty offers to take care of : He thinks in confcience that pay is due unto them, and though they merit it not at His hands, yet being refolved in His *mercy* and *goodneffe* as a *Chriftian* to pardon their fault, He will like a *King* alfo, in His *bounty* and *Honor* undertake their payment ; which none elfe (he fees) is really inclined to look after. And this He will doe, without any charge to any, fave onely to Himfelfe and His owne friends. May He but have His own Rents and Revenues returned to Him, with fome few of the *Arreares*, together with fome little part of that money which they had gotten by *Sequeftrations* and *Compofitions* from His owne party, He will undertake that the Army in few moneths fhall receive foure hundred thoufand pounds ; and if that be not fufficient, He will make up the reft by the fale of His owne Lands.

Nay, and more then all this, left *the devouring of that which is Holy, fhould prove a fnare,* and a fire to the greedy and bold adventurers, His Majefty is willing alfo to take order againft the damage of fuch perfons, and for the repayment of all fuch monies as have by them been lent upon fuch ingagements.

Nor

Nor is here all yet, His Majesty is willing to endevour the re-paration of His Enemies lost *reputations*, by suppressing and, nul-ling all Declarations and Protestations, which their own due me-rits had most justly called forth against them, and all proceedings anent any person for adhering to them.

And now what could these men (in the judgment of Reason) have desired more then was here tendred? they might have had the Authority, the whole command and power of the *Militia*; they might have possessed all the wealth to themselves which they had before, or have gotten lately, from the whole Kingdom: His Majesty would have taken the whole care of paying their *debts* and their *Servants wages*, He would have wiped them also as clean as possibly He could have done, from their black and hellish crimes of Rebellion, oppression, bloud and Treason : And He would have granted further, what ever else they could have asked, in order to their own quiet and security, would they but onely let Him come to Treat with them, and suffer His poore people *(now at length)* to enjoy an ease from war, and a free-dom from their heavy pressures.

Assuredly we may conceive those words of the Prophet, 2 *Chr.* 25. 16. to be fully appliable to these men : *God hath even deter-mined to destroy them because they have not hearkned to this counsell,* nor accepted of what was here offered to them. *Scripture* tea-cheth, that whom God purposeth to make the *power of his justice seen upon,* he infatuates, to slight and lose the opportunities of their own preservation : *Elyes* sons *hearkned not unto the voice of their Father, because the Lord would slay them* (saies the Spirit :) God did not incline their hearts to listen unto *good,* because he in-tended to cut them off for their *evils.* And such may be thought is the case and condition of these men, they have not hearkned to this voice or Message of their publike Father, because the Lords purpose is speedily to call them to a shamefull reckoning for the mischiefs they have done : many *sclaunders* and *blasphe-mies* have they cast out against his Anointed, much *peevishnesse* and *perversnesse* have they practised towards Him : much of the *innocent bloud* of their fellow-subjects and brethren have they spilt and shed, much *oppression* have they used upon them, much *hypocrisie* to deceive and cheat them of their peace and mony ; and

and much *profanation* and *despight* to that Religion and Church, wherein themselves were bred and nourished ; and that *for these things sake, the wrath of God might come* sodainly down *upon them,* as upon the most speciall *Children of disobedience,* the Lord hath *blinded their eyes* and hardened their hearts to *forsake their owne mercy,* in rejecting these motions and proffers of their Soveraign : And we believe their natures and dispositions are now so well known by these their *refusalls* so frequently iterated, by their late *Votes* or *Resolves* of *having no more to do with the King*; by their scandalous *Declaration* against His Innocency and Honour ; and by that *other* of theirs against the *Commissioners* of *Scotland,* that it will be concluded, *their hower is spent, their day is past and gone,* they shall never more meet with such advantages of preserving themselves, nor with the like tenders of grace and mercy.

Twenty daies did His Majesty (according to His wonted manner) wait their leisure for an Answer to this His so Gracious Message, and could not so much in all that time as understand from them their receipt of it ; which perversnesse and insolency in them, cannot yet cause Him to forbear again sending to them ; the welfare of His Subjects is so tender to Him, and their Happinesse so much desired by Him : yea the many and *sad complaints* of the *decay of trade,* the *dearnesse of commodities,* and the *unsupportable burden of taxes,* ecchoing daily *from divers parts of His Kingdome* into His pious and gentle ears, and threatning a *sodain failing of naturall subsistance,* will not let Him rest or desist in His endevours for peace, though Himself were to *have no share in the benefit of it,* and therefore He solicits them again in these words :

His Majesties twentieth Message.

His Majesties most gracious Message for Peace from
Carisbrooke-Castle, *Decemb.* 6. 1647.

CHARLES R.

HAd His Majesty thought it possible that His two Houses could be employed in things of greater concernment then the Peace of this miserable

ferable diftracted Kingdom ; He would have expected
with more patience, their leifure in acknowledging the
receit of his Meffage of the 16. of *November* laft. But
fince there is not in nature, any confideration preceding
to that of Peace, his Majefties conftant tenderneffe of the
welfare of his Subjects, hath fuch a prevalence with him,
that he cannot forbear the vehement profecution of a
Perfonall Treaty : which is, onely, fo much the more
defired by his Majefty, as it is fuperior to all other means
of Peace. And truly, when his Majefty confiders the feverall complaints he daily hears from all parts of this
Kingdom, That Trade is fo decayed, all Commodities
fo dear, and Taxes fo infupportable, that even naturall
fubfiftance will fodainly fail. His Majefty (to perform
the Truft repofed in him) muft ufe his uttermoft endevours for Peace, though he were to have no fhare in the
benefit of it. And hath not his Majefty done his part
for it, by devefting himfelf of fo much power & authority, as by his laft Meffage he hath promifed to do, upon
the concluding of the whole Peace ? And hath he met
with that acknowledgment from his two Houfes, which
this great Grace and Favour juftly deferves ? Surely the
blame of this great retarding of Peace muft fall fome-
where elfe, then on his Majefty.

To conclude, If ye will but confider in how little time
this neceffary good Work will be done, if you the two
Houfes will wait on his Majefty with the fame Refolutions for Peace, as he will meet you : he no way doubts,
but that ye will willingly agree to this his Majefties earneft defire of a Perfonall Treaty, and fpeedily defire his
Prefence amongft you : Where all things agreed on, being digefted into Acts (till when, it is moft unreafonable
for his Majefty or his two Houfes to defire, each of other
the

the leaft conceffion.) this Kingdom may at laft enjoy the bleffing of a long-wifht-for Peace.

From Carisbrook-Caftle, Decemb. 6. 1647.

To the Speaker of the Houfe of Peers, pro tempore, *to be communicated,&c.*

BEcaufe His Majefty herein had declared, that this *neceffary work of Peace* may be concluded in *a very little time,* were *their refolutions but like His,* and alfo affirmed, *that it would be moft unreafonable either for Himfelf or them, to defire of each other the leaft Conceffion, till things agreed on were digefted into Acts,* therefore did they make haft (more then ever they did before) to fend Him *four Bills* (fully as unconfcionable as could be devifed) to which they refolve to have His Conceffion, (as *unreafonable* a thing as He takes it to be) before He fhall get any hopes of a Treaty at their hands : By which alfo they give Him to fee and know, that how *fhort a time* foever, Himfelf fancies this *neceffary work* may be done in, yet 'tis not likely to be concluded with fuch fpeed and eafineffe : eighteen daies after this Meffage was fent, thofe Bills came to His Majefties hand, of what nature they were, that fpeech of one of thofe that fent them doth fufficiently dif-cover : *If the King figns them, He undoes Himfelf ; if He doth not, We will :* the world hath feen them, His Majefties Anfwer at four daies end unto them, was this which follows :

His Majefties twenty firft Meffage.

His Majefties moft gracious Anfwer to the Bils and Pro-pofitions prefented to Him at Carisbrook-Caftle *in the Ifle of Wight, Decemb. 24. 1647.*

CHARLS R.

THe neceffity of complying with all engaged in-terefts in thefe great diftempers, for a perfect fetlement of Peace, His Majefty finds to be none

O of

of the least difficulties He hath met with since the time of His afflictions. Which is too visible, when at the same time, that the two Houses of the English Parliament do present to his Majesty severall Bils and Propositions for His consent, the Commissioners for *Scotland* do openly protest against them. So that were there nothing in the case, but the consideration of that difference, His Majesty cannot imagine how to give such an Answer to what is now proposed, as thereby to promise Himself his great end, *A perfect Peace*. And when His Majesty farther considers, how impossible it is (in the condition He now stands) to fulfill the desires of His two Houses ; since the only ancient and known waies of passing Laws, are either by his Majesties Personall Assent in the House of Peers, or by Commission under his Great Seal of *England*: He cannot but wonder at such failings in the manner of Addresse, which is now made unto Him. Unlesse his two Houses intend, that his Majesty shall allow of a Great Seal made without his Authority, before there be any consideration had thereupon in a Treaty. Which as it may hereafter hazard the security it self; so for the present, it seems very unreasonable to his Majesty. And though his Majesty is willing to believe, that the intention of very many in both Houses, in sending these Bils before a Treaty, was only to obtain a trust from Him, and not to take any advantage by passing them to force other things from Him, which are either against His Conscience or Honour : Yet his Majesty believes it clear to all understandings, that these Bils contain (as they are now penned) not only the devesting Himself of all Soveraignty, and that without possibility of recovering it, either to Him or his Successours, (except by repeal of those Bils) but also the making his Concessions guilty of

the

the greateſt preſſures that can be made upon the Subjeƈt, as in other particulars, ſo by giving an Arbitrary and Vnlimited power to the two Houſes for ever, to raiſe and levie Forces, for Land or Sea ſervice, of what perſons (without diſtinƈtion or quality) and to what numbers they pleaſe. And likewiſe for the payment of them, to levy what Monies, in ſuch ſort, and by ſuch waies and means (and conſequently upon the Eſtates of whatſoever Perſons) they ſhall think fit & appoint. Which is utterly inconſiſtent with the Liberty & Property of the Subjeƈt, and his Majeſties truſt in proteƈting them. So that if the Major part of both Houſes, ſhall think it neceſſary to put the reſt of the Propoſitions into Bils; His Majeſty leaves all the world to judge, how unſafe it would be for Him to conſent thereunto. And if not, what a ſtrange condition (after the paſſing of theſe four Bils) his Majeſty and all his Subjeƈts would be caſt into. And here his Majeſty thinks it not unfit, to wiſh his two Houſes to conſider well the manner of their proceedíng: That when his Majeſty deſires a Perſonall Treaty with them for the ſetling of a Peace; they in anſwer, propoſe the very ſubjeƈt matter of the moſt eſſentiall part thereof to be firſt granted. A thing which will be hardly credible to Poſterity. Wherefore his Majeſty declares, That neither the deſire of being freed from this tedious and irkſome condition of life his Majeſty hath ſo long ſuffered, nor the apprehenſion of what may befall him, in caſe his two Houſes ſhal not afford him a Perſonal Treaty, ſhall make him change his reſolution, of not conſenting to any Act, till the whole Peace be concluded. Yet then, he intends not only to give juſt and reaſonable ſatisfaction in the particulars preſented to him; but alſo to make good all other Conceſſions mentioned in his Meſ

ſage

sage of the 16. of *Novemb.* last. Which he thought would have produced better effects, then what he finds in the Bils and Propositions now presented unto him.

And yet his Majesty cannot give over, but now again earnestly presseth for a Personal Treaty, (so passionately is he affected with the advantages which Peace wil bring to his Majesty and all his Subjects) of which he will not at all despair, (there being no other visible way to obtain a wel-grounded Peace.) However his Majesty is very much at ease within himself, for having fulfilled the offices both of a Christian and of a King ; and will patiently wait the good pleasure of Almighty God, to incline the hearts of his two Houses to consider their King, and to compassionate their fellow Subjects miseries.

Given at Carisbrook-Castle *in the* Isle of Wight, Decemb. 28. 1647.

For the Speaker of the Lords House pro tempore, *to be communicated to the Lords and Commons in the Parliament of* England *at* Westminster, *and the Commissioners of the Parliament of* Scotland.

HIs Majesties Afflictions have been much increased by manifesting His care (as an equall Father) that satisfaction might be given to all *ingaged interests*, therefore *Presbyterians, Independents, Army, Scots,* and all whoever they be, that acknowledge a part in them, and remain yet unsatisfied, have reason as *Christians*, as *Subjects*, as *men* for meer gratitude sake, (were there no other reason) to endeavour the *vindication* of those wrongs (at least) which His Majesty hath suffered since He stood forth as their Common Advocate. To prevent *their Audience* (upon the Kings motion) were these *Bills* devised, and sent in this sort unto His Majesty. And for His not consenting so far to their damage, and

to

to the undoing of all the reſt of His Subjects as theſe *Bils* requi-
red, was His Majeſty caſt into a more hard and miſerable Condition (by ſome degrees) then ever before ; having all His *Servants*
on the ſodain by violence thruſt out from Him, not ſo much as
one of His *Divines* allowed unto Him. Himſelf *confined* to two
or three Roomes within the walls of a loathed Priſon ; *aſſaulted*
frequently He is with evil language,and *tormented* with the ſpight-
full behaviours of the Enemy, *permitted* to ſee or ſpeak to none
but rude Souldiers, who are ſet to watch Him, and whom He
hath hourly cauſe to look upon, as Aſſaſſinates appointed for to
murder Him : His friends are not ſuffered to write unto Him, nor
His Children to ſend the remembrance of their duties, yet His
Trunks and Pockets are often ſearched for Letters, with the higheſt inſolency and rudeneſſe that can be ſhewn. And all this (with
much more of like nature then can be expreſſed) is come upon Him (as it ſeemeth) for moving in the behalf of all *ingaged in-*
tereſts : and therefore moſt truly did His Majeſty in the Beginning of this Meſſage ſay (for He hath felt it ſince) that *He found*
the complying with all ingaged intereſts in theſe great diſtempers, none
of the leaſt difficulties He met withall ſince the time of His Afflicti-
ons : and therefore alſo (as was ſaid before) were there no other
cauſe, *they* are *all* bound to ingage for Him, till they have ſet Him
free from His preſent Thraldome.

: And (indeed) the *Scotch Commiſſioners* (for their parts) began
well, in their proteſting (in the name of their whole Kingdome)
againſt thoſe unreaſonable Bils, at the ſame time, that they were
by the Engliſh Commiſſioners preſented to His Majeſty as *being*
prejudiciall to Religion, to the Crown, to the union, and intereſt of both
Nations, and directly different from their former mutuall procee-
dings and ingagements : now His Majeſty for taking notice of this
(which was uttered in His preſence and in the name of a whole
Kingdome) is extreamly quarrelled at : and becauſe He did not
ſigne the ſaid *Bils* (notwithſtanding the ſaid *proteſt*) He is immediately made cloſe Priſoner, and ſenſible of more then barbarous uſage : the Method of which is in part expreſſed, in the following *Declaration,* which twenty daies after His cloſe confine-
ment was written by His Majeſties own hand, and ſome twenty
daies after that, by the ſpeciall order and providence of him who

is

is *the preserver of Princes* brought to light, and publifhed to our
view : if any of His people can read or heare the fame without
melting hearts and yearning bowels towards their King, and in-
flamed fpirits againft thefe tormenters of Him, aſſuredly they
may be fufpected to have nothing of Chrift, or goodneſſe in them.

The Kings Declaration from Carisbrook-Caftle, Jan. 18. 1647.

To all my people of whatfoever Nation, Quality or Condition.

AM I thus laid afide, and muft I not fpeak for my
felfe ? No ! I will fpeak, and that to all my
People, (which I would have rather done, by the
way of my two Houfes of Parliament, but that there is
a publike Order, neither to make addreſſes to, or receive Meſſage from me) and who but you can be judge
of the differences betwixt Me, and my two Houfes ?
I know none elfe ; for I am fure, you it is, who will enjoy the happineſſe, or feel the mifery, of good, or ill Government ; And we all pretend who fhould run fafteft to
ferve you ; without having a regard (at leaft in the firft
place) to particular Interefts : And therefore I defire
you to confider the ftate I am, and have bin, in, this long
time, and whether my Actions have more tended to the
Publick, or my owne particular good ; for whofoever
will look upon me, barely, as I am Man, without that
liberty (which the meaneft of my Subjects enjoyes) of
going whither, and converfing with whom I will : As a
Husband and Father, without the comfort of my Wife
and Children ; or laftly, as a King, without the leaft
fhew of Authority or Power, to protect my diftreſſed
Subjects ; Muft conclude me, not only void of all Na-

turall

turall Affection, but alfo to want common underftanding ; if I fhould not moft cheerfully embrace the readi-
eft way, to the fettlement of thefe diftracted Kingdoms :
As alfo on the other fide, doe but confider the forme
and draught of the Bils lately prefented unto me, and
as they are the conditions of a Treaty, ye will conclude,
that the fame fpirit which hath ftill been able to fruftrate
all my fincere and conftant endeavours for Peace, hath
had a powerfull influence on this Meffage ; for though
I was ready to grant the fubftance, and comply with
what they feeme to defire ; yet as they had framed it, I
could not agree thereunto, without deeply wounding
my Confcience and Honour, and betraying the truft repofed in me, by abandoning my People to the Arbitrary
and Vnlimited Power of the two Houfes for ever, for the
leavying and maintaining of Land or Sea Forces, without diftinction of quality, or limitation for Mony taxes :
And if I could have paffed them in termes ; how unheard-of a condition were it for a Treaty, to grant before-
hand the moft confiderable part of the fubject matter ?
How ineffectuall were that debate like to prove, wherein
the moft potent Party had nothing of moment left to
aske ; and the other nothing more to give ? So confe-
quently, how hopeleffe of mutuall complyance ? Without which, a fettlement is impoffible : Befides, if after
my conceffions, the two Houfes fhould infift on thofe
things, from which I cannot depart ; how defperate
would the condition of thefe Kingdomes be, when the
moft proper and approved remedy fhould become ineffectuall ? Being therefore fully refolved that I could
neither in Confcience, Honour, or Prudence, paffe thofe
foure B ls ; I onely endeavour'd to make the Reafons
and Juftice of my Denyall appeare to all the world, as
                                                    they,

they doe to Me, intending to give as little diſ-ſatisfacti-
on to the two Houſes of Parliament, (without betraying
my own Cauſe) as the matter would beare : I was deſi-
rous to give my Anſwer, of the 28. of *December* laſt, to
the Commiſſioners Sealed, (as I had done others heretofore, and ſometimes at the deſire of the Commiſſioners)
chiefly , becauſe when my Meſſages or Anſwers were
publickly known, before they were read in the Houſes ;
prejudiciall interpretations were forced on them, much
differing, and ſometimes contrary to my meaning : For
example, my Anſwer from *Hampton-court* , was accuſed
of dividing the two Nations , becauſe I promiſed to
give ſat sfaction to the *Scots*, in all things concerning that
Kingdome : And this laſt ſuffers in a contrary ſenſe, by
making me intend to intereſt *Scotland* in the Lawes of
this Kingdome, (then which nothing was, nor is, further
from my thoughts) becauſe I took notice of the *Scots*
Commiſſioners proteſting againſt the Bils and Propoſitions, as contrary to the intereſts and engagements of
the two Kingdomes : Indeed, if I had not mentioned
their diſſent ; an Objection, not without ſome probability, might have been made againſt me, both in reſpect
the *Scots* are much concern'd in the Bill for the Militia,
and in ſeverall other Propoſitions ; and my ſilence
might, with ſome Juſtice, have ſeemed to approve of it :
But the Commiſſioners refuſing to receive my Anſwer
Sealed, I (upon the engagement of their, and the Gover-
nors Honour, that no other uſe ſhould be made, or notice taken of it, then as if it had not been ſeen) read and
delivered it open unto them ; Whereupon, what hath
ſince paſſed , either by the Governour, in diſcharging
moſt of my Servants, redoubling the Guards, and reſtrai-
ning me of my former liberty, (and all this, as himſelfe
                                                    confeſt,

confeft, meerly out of his owne diflike of my Anfwer, notwithftanding his beforefaid Engagement) or afterwards, by the two Houfes, (as the Governour affirmes) in confining me within the circuit of this Caftle, I appeale to God and the World, whether my faid Anfwer deferved the reply of fuch proceedings : befides the unlawfulneffe for Subjects to imprifon their King : That, by the permiffion of Almighty God, I am reduced to this fad condition, as I no way repine, fo I am not without hope, but that the fame God, will, in due time, convert thefe Afflictions into my advantage : in the meane time, I am confident to beare thefe croffes with patience, and a great equality of Minde : but by what meanes or occafion I am come to this Relapfe in my Affaires, I am utterly to feek, efpecially when I confider, that I have facrificed, to my two Houfes of Parliament, for the Peace of the Kingdome, all, but, what is much more deare to me then my Life, *My Confcience and Honour* ; defiring nothing more, then to performe it, in the moft proper and naturall way, *A Perfonall Treaty.* But that which makes me moft at a loffe, is, the remembring my fignall complyance with the Army, and their interefts ; and of what importance my Complyance was to them ; and their often repeated Profeffions and Ingagements, for my juft Rights, in generall, at *Newmarket* and S. *Albans* ; and their particular explanation of thofe generals, by their Voted and Re-voted Propofals ; which I had reafon to underftand fhould be the utmoft extremity would be expected from me, and that, in fome things therein, I fhould be eafed ; (herein appealing to the Confciences of fome of the chiefeft Officers in the Army, if what I have faid, be not punctually true) and how I have failed of their expectations, or my profeffions to them ;

P   I

I challenge them and the whole World to produce the leaft colour of Reafon. And now I would know, what it is that is defired : Is it Peace ? I have fhewed the way (being both willing, and defirous to performe my part in it) which is, a juft compliance with all chiefe interefts : Is it Plenty and Happineffe ? they are the infeperable effects of Peace : Is it Security ? I, who wifh that all men would forgive and forget like Me, have offered the *Militia* for my time : Is it Liberty of Confcience ? He who wants it, is moft ready to give it : Is it the right adminiftration of Juftice ? Officers of truft are committed to the choice of my two Houfes of Parliament : Is it frequent Parliaments ? I have legally, fully concurr'd therewith : Is it the Arrears of the Army ? upon a fettlement, they will certainly be payed with much eafe ; but before, there will be found much difficulty, if not impoffibility in it.

Thus all the world cannot but fee my reall and unwearied endeavours for Peace, the which (by the grace of God) I fhall neither repent me of, nor ever be flackned in, notwithftanding my paft, prefent, or future, fufferings ; but, if I may not be heard, let every one judge, who it is that obftructs the good I would, or might doe : What is it that men are afraid to hear from me ? It cannot be Reafon, (at leaft, none will declare themfelves fo unreafonable, as to confeffe it) and it can leffe be, impertinent or unreafonable Difcourfes ; for thereby, peradventure I might more juftifie this my Reftraint, then the caufers themfelves can do ; fo that, of all wonders yet this is the greateft to me : but, it may be eafily gathered, how thofe men intend to govern, who have ufed me thus : And if it be my hard Fate to fall together with the liberty of this Kingdome, I fhall not blufh for my felfe, but much

la-

lament the future miſeries of my People ; the which, I ſhall ſtill pray to God to avert ; what ever becomes of me.   *CHARLES R.*

BEhold here all *Engliſh-men,* and you of *Scotland, Wales,* and *Ireland,* in whoſe manly Breaſts doth yet remain any true ſparks of right Religion, or Auncient Honour : *Behold your King,* the breath of your Noſtrils, the Anointed of the Lord, under whoſe ſhadow you dwelt in peace, injoying wealth many years together, whoſe yoak was eaſie and ſweet unto you, Behold, behold, He is taken, and ſnared in a pit, ſee how ſadly He *ſits in darkneſſe and hath no light* ; hearken how He complains unto you, out of Priſon, that *He is layed aſide,* or, *become like a broken veſſel :* forgotten (as it were) *like a dead man out of mind :* ſhall it be as nothing to you(All you to whom this Appeal is made,this Declaration ſent ; *)* that your Protector, your Defender, the Glory of Chriſtians, and Mirrour of Kings is thus uſed ? Have you no feeling of His ſufferings ? no ſhare in His ſorrows ? is it not for your ſakes, that He indures all theſe hard and heavy things ? can there be named any other reaſon for them, then becauſe He will not yeild you up to be ſlaves and bond-men ? is He not diveſted of all His power, ſtript of His whole Authority, deprived of all His Comforts, barr'd from the ſight of Wife and Children, denied Liberty of going whither, and converſing with whom He deſires; becauſe He will not conſent that you without rule or reaſon, ſhould be handled and uſed in this manner ? He will not wound His Conſcience and Honour in betraying the truſt repoſed in Him by Almighty God over you ; He will not deliver you up into thoſe hands, which have already ſo much abuſed you ; He will not abandon you to the *unlimited power of the two Houſes for ever :* He will not grant them His leave, *to levy Land and Sea forces* from *among you* by violence, and to maintain them continually *upon you,* at your coſt and Charges, and *againſt you,* to keep you under, without either Law or Limitation : in a word, He will not conſent that you ſhould be kept in perpetuall Beggery, and made *Vaſſals* to your equals and fellows ; and for this cauſe are all theſe miſeries heaped on Him.

P 2   Read

Read over again, and view well, *His* many Gracious Messages,
and *offers* together with *their* unreasonable *demands* and Propositions ; and remember withall , how uncomfortably, how charge-
ably, nay how miserably every way, you have lived, since these
men (who would alwaies rule) have exercised power over you.
Oh *how is your Gold become dim*, since your King hath bin in darknesse ? *How is your fine Gold changed*, since He hath been excluded ? *the pretious stones of the Sanctuary*, how have they been de-
filed, made as Common, and poured out in every street, since He
the *most pretious* of all, hath been refused by these new *Mushrom
Master-Builders?* the most Honourable Sons of *Sion*, the Children
of your Princes, *comparable to fine Gold*, how are they esteemed
in these daies *as earthen pitchers* ? how have your most Heroick
Nobles been vilified and debased ; your most Gallant *Gentry* been
trod and trampled under ? Your free-borne *Yeomanry*, the sinews
of the Kingdome, how have they been tyranniz'd over in their
own houses, and how many of all sorts have been begger'd, but-
cher'd, and destroy'd, since these unhappy men (who would for
ever sit aloft) have domineered ? How hath the most reverend &
learned *Clergie*, the servants of the most high God, been despised,
persecuted, and defamed ? How is that rich and renowned City,
London, become as a *Widow*, in the absence of her Husband, by the
meanes and operation of these new *usurpers* ? How hath her most
eminent *Magistrates*, her *Maiors*, and *Aldermen* been imprisoned ?
Her wealthy *Merchants* impoverished , her *Commons* of all sorts
been baffled, and deluded ? How hath the lustre of her excellent
order, and flourishing *government* been darkned and obscured ?
She was so great among the *Nations*, (while her Soveraignes influence shined upon her) that for her Beauty ; Freedome, and
Splendour above the rest, she was reckoned a *Princesse* among all
the *European* Provinces, being as rich in Treasures, as she was in
People : But now, alas ! how is she become a *Captive*, and a *Tri-
butary* to her owne servants ? *She now weepeth sore*, (at least she
hath cause so to doe, and that as well in regard of her deception,
and her sin, as of her misery) for that *among all her lovers*, (whom
she so foolishly, and so wickedly doted on) *she hath none to comfort her :* for all those her friends whom she trusted in, *have dealt
treacherously with her*, and are become her enemies, yea her most
                                                                vexatious

vexatious Tormenters : And becaufe our moft Chriftian King is not willing to figne *a Bill of perpetuity;* for the continuation of thefe fad Calamities upon her, upon you, and upon us all for ever; therefore is He tortured in that manner as we fee and hear : therfore is His Princely Honour blafted; His Royall good name defamed, His Regall power, Authority, and Revenues taken away and kept from Him ; His pious Confcience affaulted, His facred perfon imprifoned, and every day in danger to be maffacred, and murdered. O may it not well be asked and faid, *Was there ever forrow, like unto his forrow,* for fuch a caufe ? Were there ever wrongs like unto thefe that are done unto our King , becaufe He will not confent to the utter undoing of us his people ? Affuredly; never was people more wretched, and accurfed then we fhall be, (and that meritoriouſly) both of God and Men, if we fuffer this, and doe not ftand up and appeare for His deliverance.

For what are *thefe men* that thus tyrannize over our Soveraign, and over us ? are they not his *vaffals,* and our *fellowes,* nay our *fervants* entrufted by us, to manifeft and prefent the tenders of our duty and reverence unto him ; and doth it not concerne us therefore, to bring them to correction, (as the cafe now ftands with the King) for thefe their groffe enormities ; will not their impieties, and exorbitancies elfe be laid to our charge ? Nay, doe they not in their *impudencie* act all their wickedneffes in our names ? would they not have their late defamatory Libell to be underftood as the expreffion of our fenfes ? Doe they not call it *The Declaration of the Commons,* (fcil. of *England,* as if we (at leaft) gave allowance to it, or fet them awork to make it ? When, as God and our confciences doe beare us witneffe, we loathe it with our very foules, as the moft horrid heap of the moft fhameleffe lies, blafphemies and flanders, that ever was fpued up againft Majefty and Innocencie by men or devils, fince the firft Creation. Nay, have they not fince their publication of it, tempted and provoked many of the ignorant of us; in divers Countries, to fet our Hands to Papers coyned *by* themfelves, of Gratulations *to* themfelves, for venting the fame, and for making thofe their wicked Votes againft our Soveraigne, the Lords Anointed ? Doe they not hereby plainly endeavour (Satan-like) to involve our foules in their owne guilt, and to plunge them for ever in the fame pit of damnation with

them-

themselves ? As if it were not enough that they have already wasted us all, in our estates ; and wounded the consciences of too many of us, by ingaging us (through their false pretences of *Religion, Liberty*, and *Privilege of Parliament*) to associate with them in this unnaturall War, unlesse they doe this also : And have they not menaced others of us, because we refused to approve of this their late most abominable wickednesse, and went about rather to move for His Majesties Liberty and restoration ? Have they not threatned to plunder and sequester us of all we have yet remaining, if we proceeded to make any motions or requests to that purpose ? as if they had a spight and malice at Almighty God himselfe, for opening our eyes at length, and bringing us out of that darknesse, wherein they had shut us, and hoped alwayes to keep us : and for his touching our hearts with remorse and sorrow, for our former complyance with them, as if also we must never dare to speak more, but onely such words as they shall suggest, and put into our mouthes ; nor to set our hands unto any thing but what they (forsooth) shall frame and dictate to us ; And is this the *Freedome of the Subject* so much cryed up ? Is this the *Liberty* which the people of *England* have so fought for ? Is this our so flourishing state of happinesse which was promised by our blessed Reformers ? *Sero sapiunt phryges*, fooles may grow wise at length, and so from henceforth shall we, for ever following them any farther, or being guided by them any more, who by their glorious *professions* and *protestations* have seduced us already so far from the wayes of God.

We cannot but call to mind, the *proceedings* of this Palliament, (or of this *Thing* which so calls it selfe, being in very deed, but a *corrupt faction* in it :) How at first they framed a *Protestation Generall*, for the *matter* of it good, (we still confesse and acknowledge) but the deep subtilty and *intrigo* of it, was not then apparent to us : But now we consider how they did (without the Kings sanction and ratification) little lesse then *impose* it upon the whole Kingdome, whereby they slily crept into a kind of unexampled authority, no way belonging to them ; which they cunningly masked, under the specious pretences of pious respects to the *Protestant Religion*, Loyall regards to *His Majesties Person and Dignity*, and of their serious care of the *Priviledges of Parliament*,

Pro-

Properties and Liberties of the Subject: no one of which (as we now fee by their actions) was ever in their thoughts to preferve, for their whole endeavours have fince been, and ftil are, to deftroy and fuppreffe all thefe: but hereby at firft they catch'd us in their net, and carryed us downe the ftreame with them.

And having thus furprifed *us,* Jealoufies and Fears prefently began to furprize *them*; which alfo the whole Kingdome muft be fenfible of, as if all the things to be defended by the *Proteftation* were in fome eminent danger of fodaine deftruction: to prevent which a *Petition* is framed in all hafte by themfelves, and fent downe into all Countries to be fubfcribed there, and fent back as the unanimous defire of the whole Kingdome, *that Bifhops and Popifh Lords,* (who muft be apprehended the conjoynt and deadly enemies to all good things contained in the Proteftation) *might be put out of Parliament; that the Kingdome might be put into a pofture of defence* (or war) *againft them* and their Complices; and the better to colour and credit thebufineffe, we muft defire in the fame Petition *to have a monethly faft Authorized.* And we well remember, there was care taken at that very time; (left this *miftery of Iniquity* that was in working fhould be difcovered to us:) that the Learned *Seers,* or *watchmen* of God (who were moft likely to to make it known,) fhould be expofed to fcorne and contempt, under the name of *Prelaticall, Scandalous,* and *Malignant Clergie*; that fo their Teftimonies might be of no efteeme with us; and a generation of men full of ignorance, covetoufneffe or difcontents, were countenanced and advanced over us, as fitly inftrumentall and fubfervient to the defigne on foot, which (now we finde) was only to ruine our King, and us.

The Confequents of this *Petition* appeared foon after to be thefe. 1. An alteration or change of military Officers, the Train-Bands being committed into the hands onely of fuch as were called *Confiding men.* 2. The appointment of a Guard to defend our *worthies of Parliament,* (as they were entitled.) And 3. An expofall of the Kings Perfon and Government to all poffible danger and difgrace: And that 1. By a moft *fcandalous Remonftrance,* wherein the fins of themfelves and others (who had been His ill Officers) were all layed to His Charge. 2. By fetting the *Tumultuous People* upon Him, to drive Him from *Weftminfter.*

And

And then 3. By raising *an Army* to fetch Him back again, as was pretended, though in very deed we finde now, it was to destroy Him rather.

We remember how they told us then, that *the King was amongst them in His politick Capacity*; whereby they had full power to act, even as if He had been personally there; but if He were suffered to be absent, He would doubtlesse in *His naturall Capacity* be very mischievous to the Kingdome; having such ill Councellours about Him, (as they said He had) and such damned Cavaliers, who (as their preachers taught us to beleeve for good Doctrine) were as bad as devills; and whose very shapes and faces *the Lord* (*in his judgement*) *had already so altered, that they did not now look like men, as formerly, but like strange horrid monsters:* So that God having set a visible mark of His vengeance upon them, as He did on *Cain;* our duty was, and we were bound in Conscience to pursue them as *Reprobates,* and as men cursed of God, unlesse our selves would runne the hazard of that *bitter Curse* which was layed upon the *Inhabitants of* Meroz, *because they did not help the Lord against the Mighty.* After this manner they seduced us, and led us, (too many of us) to think ill of the King, and of those that were Conscientious and faithfull unto Him.

Having thus consorted themselves with His Majesty in the Empire, by their incroaching on His Authority; and thus gulled us by this device of His *Politick* and *naturall Capacity;* (as if being arm'd or Authorized by the *one,* we might destroy him in the *other:*) Which distinction, we now understand (since the returne of Reason to us) to be but a meer vaporous Fancy, a grosse Bull, a very absurd Juggle, invented by state Empericks to cheat silly people into disorder and disobedience.

And we are confident, if we shall now goe about to pay them the interest of this their distinction, and make it good upon themselves, (as indeed we ought to endeavour for in such a case onely; it may goe for currant) themselves would be directly of our opinion: Should we but tell them, that we consider of them two wayes, in a *Politick,* and in a *Naturall* capacity: As they are in the first, we honour and worship them; we love them, and regard them, as they are members of the *Body Politick Representa-*
tive;

tive ; but (by their favours) in their *naturall Capacity*, as they are men, we intend to order and handle them as *Rebels, Traytors, parricides, fratricides, thieves, and murderers* use to be dealt with-all, even according to Law and Juſtice, and the due deſert of their owne merits : let them aske their own hearts whether in ſuch a caſe, and at ſuch a time they will readily approve of it.

But hereby (as we were ſaying) they began to raiſe Forces in the *name of King and Parliament* ; and under that ſtile (or rather Contradiction) Commiſſions are iſſued, Souldiers are levied, and Taxes of divers ſorts and unheard-of names impoſed upon us the Kings Subjects ; to fight againſt and oppreſſe our King, (as we now perceive) and to take His Regall power directly from Him : for they are not aſhamed now to publiſh (in plain Engliſh) be-fore all the world, that this Warre was undertaken to wreſt the *Militia* and *Legiſlative power* from the King and His Poſterity : In the 64. pag. of their late *Declaration againſt the Scots*, (or con-cerning the Papers of *the Scots Commiſſioners :*) their words to this purpoſe are theſe, *The Kingdome of Scotland* (ſay they) *inga-ged with us, in this war, upon theſe Principles,* viz. *for to have the Le-giſlative power, and the exerciſe of the Militia, without, and againſt the Kings conſent.*

If the *Kingdome of Scotland* did *engage* with them, on theſe terms, and for theſe ends (as they now tell us) yet we are confi-dent that the people of *England*, were better inſtructed then to do ſo, for *they had not ſo learned Chriſt,* who commands to *give unto Cæſar, the things that are Cæſars,* and not to take them away from Him. We were here told of no other cauſes of the war, then to maintain *Proteſtant Religion,* eſtabliſhed in this Church, to *defend the Kings Perſon, Honour, and Eſtate,* and to *free Him from ill Counſellours,* and to preſerve the *Priviledges of Parliament,* the *Laws of the Land,* and *Liberties of the Subject,* and to *bring De-linquents to puniſhment,* all which we were aſſured (and that from the Pulpit too) as well as from the Parliament and the Preſſe, were lawfull cauſes for a War ; though now we ſee how we were abuſed in that alſo, for Chriſtian verity gives warrant to none of them, unleſſe withall, we have the *call* and allowance of the *Su-pream Authority.* Yea and beſides, how many times did theſe *Declarers* proteſt before all the world, that *it was not in their*

thoughts,

114 *His Majesties most Gracious*

thoughts, *to loosen the reines of Government, or to diminish any of the Kings rights:* no, *we professe* (said they) *in the fight of Almighty God, which is the strongest obligation of a Christian, &c. that no ill Affection to His Majesties Person, no designe to the prejudice of His just Honour and Authority, ingaged us to raise Forces, and to take up Armes.* And again, *We professe from our very hearts and souls, but Loyalty and Obedience to His Crown, our readinesse and resolution to defend His Person, and support His estate with our lives and fortunes to the uttermost of our powers:* And again oftentimes, *God deal so by them, as they intended to make Him terrible to His Enemies abroad, and glorious among His friends at home, &c.* And yet now they tell the world (after all this) *that they ingaged at the very first in this War to have the Legiflative power, and the exercise of the Militia, without and against the Kings consent:* and they say *the Scots ingaged with them herein*; which we scarce believe, for we know the *Scots* are too *politick* and *wise a Nation*, then not to foresee their own damage, if the *Legiflative power*, and the *Militia* of this Kingdome, should be wrested out of the hands of the King, their Country-man and Soveraign; and put solely into the hands of those, who have no such relations or Affections to them. And (beside) the *Scots Commissioners* had said, (as these their opposers do alleage in the same *page*) that *they were obliged by their Covenant, Allegiance, and Duty of Subjects, not to diminish, but to support the Kings just Power and Greatnesse:* and therefore, we have reason to believe, they did not intend the Contrary at the beginning, and the rather, because *these men* say they did, whom we never yet found true in any thing.

    Indeed, in Answer to that of the Scots Commissioners, they affirm (though without proof or reason) that *the King Contrary to His Oath, had diminished the just Priviledges of Parliament, and Liberties of the Subjects*; *and how* (fay they) *can He that breaks down the hedge, complain of incroachment upon His severall?* so that the Kings pretended incroachment on them, is now become a warrant for them to incroach really upon Him; and to take away *all* His Kingly power from Him, only because (by their own sole testimony) He had made a *diminution* of somewhat that belonged to them. This is good Parliament Divinity, as the world goes in these daies, fetched sure out of the *Turks Alchoran,* or else

elſe from among the *Savage Heathens* in *New England*; for no *Proteſtant*, no true *Chriſtian*, nor no *Parliament* before this, did ever allow or connive at it, much leſſe urge or alleage it, to warrant themſelves in the practice of it.

But we cannot paſſe by, without obſervation, how they prove their fore-mentioned Charge againſt the *Scots* in the ſame *page, Some of theſe very Commiſſioners* (ſay they) *were amongſt the forwardeſt, to ingage the Kingdoms in a joynt War upon the Principles fore-named* (*viz.* to exerciſe the Legiſlative power, and Militia without and againſt the Kings conſent) *alſo in Oaths and Covenants to be impoſed on both Kingdoms, in Taxes to raiſe Mony upon them, taking away the Book of Common Prayer and eſtabliſhing the Directory inſtead thereof, and in divers other things, wherein the higheſt exerciſe of the Legiſlative power doth conſiſt.* Theſe be their Arguments, whereby they ſpeak themſelves to be as bad *Logitians,* as they are *Chriſtians.* Their doings *ſince* they began, are alleaged as Reaſons to prove *why* they began: and their unjuſt Actions in their progreſſe, are made the grounds and warrants of and for their ungodly undertaking.

But did any of thoſe *Oaths* and *Covenants,* (which were impoſed on both or either of the Kingdoms) mention the cauſe of the war or of peoples ingagement to be, for *to take the Legiſlative power and the Militia totally from the King, and to have it exerciſed without and againſt His conſent?* if any ſuch matters had been expreſſed, we are very confident, they would have had but few either *Engliſh* or *Scots,* joyning in Covenant with them, or lending their Aſſiſtance.

But in *pag.66.* of the ſame *Declaration,* they would fain ſuggeſt, that though there be no *Reaſon,* yet there is ſome *likelyhood* of *Reaſonableneſſe,* in this their injuſtice, and wrongfull dealings, in taking the *Legiſlative Power* and *Militia* from the King: for they argue thus:

It is much more likely (ſay they) *that a King ſhould be miſtaken, then the Great Councell of the Kingdom, and that a King ſhould ſtop that which is for the good of the whole Kingdome, then that the whole Kingdome repreſented in Parliament ſhould deſire what ſhould be for their own hurt: And 'tis much more likely, that a King ſhould make uſe of one of His Kingdoms to oppreſſe another, that He might make*

Himſelf

Himself absolute over all (if He hath the *Militia and Power* in His hand,) then that He should (with the same) hinder one Kingdome to wrong another, or all the Subjects of a Kingdome to wrong themselves.

We do very well remember, that many of us (the Common people of *England)* were befooled with these their *likelyhoods* at the beginning, for they used these very expreffions *then* unto us : but we can now anfwer them from our own experience, better then we could at that time do : and we fay, *'tis much more certain* that a King hath been, is, and will be, much more *tender of the bloud* of His Subjects, much more *indulgent of the wealth* of His people, much more *carefull to maintain* and preferve them in their Rights, and to keep them from oppreffing one another, then thofe are, or have been who now call themfelves *the Great Councell of the Kingdome.* We are fure, *there are more of a Parents bowels in Him,* (for we have felt them) *then there is of Brotherly affection in them, towards us,* (which we have had fome feeling of too, though to our grief and forrow.) And therefore we can and muft conclude, that *the Subjects are far more happy every way, and free from being oppreffed by one another, under the fatherly Government of a King, then under the tyranous ufurpation of fellow-fubjects :* for we now remember that God hath promifed in exprefs words, to guide the King fo, *that his lips fhall not tranfgreffe in Judgment :* but we find no fuch promife made to a *Parliament,* that refolves to act *without,* and *againft their Kings* confent : we know that Scripture faith, *the Kings heart is in Gods hand,* and from thence we now believe it was, that His Government was fo juft and gentle ; but the Actions and behaviours of thefe men hath fully perfwaded us, that *their Hearts be in the Devils hand,* whereby it hath come to paffe, that their purpofes and their practices have been fo bloudy, fo mifchievous, and fo deftructive.

And yet *thefe men* fuppofing (as it feems) that we are all as bruit Beafts, in refpect of themfelves (having *no underftanding* at all, but muft fubmit ftill to be held in, *with their Bits and Bridles,)* do declare, that *the Militia is the foundation of fecurity to them and to their pofterity ;* as if we were all bound to believe, and had reafon for it, that their *bleffed felves,* and *their precious pofterity,* were rather to be fecured and preferved thereby, then the King and

His :

His : and in *page 70.* they argue as *Rabsaketh* did, from their successe, that God favoured their unrighteous doings, and was *even
such another as themselves,* directly of their opinion ; *the dispute
(*say they*) concerning the Militia, hath been long, and sadly debated
both in black and red letters, but God himself hath now given the ver-
dict on our side.*

And in the very same place they tell all us English-men (as if
the Militia had never yet been in His Majesties hand, or we had
quite forgotten our freedome, happinesse and prosperity under
Kingly Government) *that our Magna Charta, our Courts of Justice, our High Court of Parliament it self, our Lives, Liberties and
Estates ; that we are not all at the will of one man ; that the King cannot make Laws, nor raise Monies without consent of Parliament ;
and that all Offenders may be punished in Courts of Justice ; all this
(* say they *) signifies nothing at all to us, if the Militia by Sea and
Land be in the King alone, we are all absolute slaves, and by so much
in a worse Condition because we think our selves at Liberty.* All this
of theirs doth but shew us, what opinion they have of us, for our
giving so much credit to them heretofore ; But truly we shall de-
serve to be *their absolute slaves* for ever, (as they would have us)
and to be branded to all posterity for *absolute fools* too, and for
the *rankest Cowards* that ever were, if this their Language (were
there nothing else) should not fill us up, with high disdain against
them, and make us resolve never to desist, till we have made them
know both themselves and us better.

And to awaken our spirits more yet, let us hear what they say
further in the same place to our conceived *simplicities. How ridi-
culous (*say they*) are those Laws which may be violated by force, and
by force not be defended :* (who hath violated our Laws by force
but themselves ? and who hath been the defender of them but
the King whose Laws they are ?) *And what a mock Authority
(*say they*) is that of Courts of Justice, and of the High Court of Parliament it self, if it be not accompanied with the power of the sword,
when by the power of the sword it shall be opposed, affronted, resisted,
their summons scorned, their Messengers kicked about the streets,
their Votes and Judgments derided.* A mock-Authority indeed that
is, and a *mock-Parliament* too that disclaims Him, from whom it
self derives its being, and to whom *God* and the *Law* hath committed the power of the Sword. We

We have had heretofore many Parliaments, but never read or heard of any, while they kept their integrity, and adhered to their maker, that conven'd them together, who were ever *opposed, affronted, resisted,* or had any of *their summons scorned, their Messengers kicked about the streets, or their Votes and Judgements derided:* therefore all this is but *copia verborum,* some flowers of Rebellious Rhetorick, whereby they thinke to keep silly fools, (such as they take us still to be) in that vile Captivity unto themselves, wherein they formerly had, and led us.

Yea and pag. 73. of that their so *bonny Declaration,* they tell us to the everlasting comfort both of us, and of our purses; that tis necessary that their Armies be kept still on foot, even so long as themselves, and their posterities shall sit, which they make account shall be but *in perpetuum,* from *Generation to Generation* till the worlds end: their words are these, *for the Parliaments consulting freely, and acting securely it will be necessary (as we have ever done since the War) to keep up forces; which were they all disbanded (as the Scotch Commissioners desire) we should not long consult freely and act securely:* They mean sure in cutting our throats, in banishing, imprisoning, and hanging our persons, in sequestring our estates, in oppressing, plundering, and taking from us our goods and fortunes, in destroying our Religion, peace, and order, for nothing else do we know they have *consulted* about, or *acted* since they first raised their *Forces,* or begun their war; we have had *Parliaments* before now, that have behaved themselves a great deale better, then these *Declarers* have done; that have *consulted* better, and *acted* better every way; and yet never thought it necessary, either to raise or keep up *Forces* for their owne guard or safety: No, for they were fenc'd with *Innocency,* and *Noblenesse of Spirit;* with their *owne uprightnesse and their Countries Love,* which together with the Guard of God, and his Angels, was their Protection; they desired no other *Militia* then *Faith* and a *good Conscience* to secure them. For why, they had never bath'd themselves in their Countries bloud, nor foul'd their hands with oppression, nor any way deserved the *odium* of their Nation. But these men shew what *they* have merited by their fears; and discover, that as they raised Forces at first, *to subdue the King,* so they intend now to keep them up *to subdue the Kingdome,* and to keep those

in

in low slavery, whose help they have had against Him: and so they will pay their servants, (for as such onely they account those whom they have imployed or made use of) *à la mode du diable*; in that manner as Satan rewards those that work for him.

And now the world sees at *last*, who began the war at *first*, and hears from them who know best, what was the true cause thereof; *even to wrest the Legislative power, and the Militia out of the Kings hands, and to excercise the same without and against His consent.* How true their former clamours have been, that *the King first tooke up Armes against the Parliament; and that the Parliament was only on the defensive part,* let the very seduced part of men now judge. His sacred Majesty in his great wisdome saw this to be their end at first, and told the world of it, but could not be heard or beleeved, so loud a noise was made to the contrary: themselves (in the 68. pag. of that their Declaration) tell the *Scotch* Commissioners (who had said, *it was contrary to their judgements and Oath of Allegeance to divest the Crown, the King and His Posterity of the right and power of the Militia*) that *they fortifie their opinion with the very same Arguments, and almost in the very same words, as the King did at the beginning of this war, in His Declarations,* whereby they acknowleged, that His Majesty even then, had spoken to that purpose. It is hoped therefore, that all men doe now apprehend, who they are that (all this while) have been the *Deceivers*.

Againe, the world also hath now seen, how far and wherein His Majesty hath been averse to peace, since the beginning of the war: He would not hitherto be either forced or perswaded to resigne up wholly and for ever unto them, that which from the very first they resolved to have from Him; *the Legislative power, and the Militia of the Kingdome to be exercised without and against Himself,* to the perpetuall enslavement and thraldome of all us His poor Subjects; whom God hath committed to his trust to protect and defend; And therefore (if it were lawfull for Subjects upon any occasion to imprison their King) yet what great cause or substantiall reason these have had to do so, or to use their Soveraigne as they have done, to resolve to make no more addresses, or applications to Him, let the world judge.

And from these many gracious Messages of His Majesty for

peace, thus flighted, contemned, and defpifed by them, let their little modefty and candour, or rather their great fhamelefneffe and impudency be obferved in their making the *foundation* of their *impious Votes*, to be *His averfeneffe unto peace*, and in beginning their *Declaration* againft Him in that manner as they have done: *viz.* in thefe words:

How fruitleffe our former Addreffes have been to the King, is fo well known to the world that it may be expected we fhall now declare, why we made the laft, or fo many before, rather then why we are refolved to make no more.

We cannot acknowledge any great confidence, that our words could have been more verfwafive with Him, then Sighs and groanes ; the Tears and crying Blood (an heavy crie) the Blood of Fathers, Brothers, and Children at once, the Blood of many hundred thoufand Free-borne Subjects in Three great Kingdomes, which cruelty it felf could not but pity to deftroy.

We muft not be fo unthankefull to God as to forget we were never forced to any Treaty; and yet we have no leffe then feven times made fuch Applications to the King, and tendred fuch Propofitions, that might occafion the world to judge, we have not onely yeelded up our wils and Affections, but our Reafon alfo and judgement , for obtaining any true Peace or Accommodation. But it never yet pleafed the King to accept of any Tender fit for us to make, nor yet to offer any fit for us to receive.

Be judges in this cafe, (O all ye people of the World) now you have read and feen what *offers* and *tenders* the King hath made, what reafon thefe men had thus to 'peale Him ? thinke you not they are men of credit, worthy to be trufted another time, fit to be beleeved in all they fay further in the fequele of their *Declaration*, fith their modefty and truth is fuch in the firft page of it? Affuredly you cannot that conclude, but *this* of *theirs* is the moft groundleffe, fhamelesse, malicious, and impudent flander, that ever was printed, (by fuch an Authority as is pretended) againft fuch a Perfon : And a *Lye* (pardon that *Scotch* word) fo *groffe*, and fo *thick* that like *the darkeneffe of Ægypt*, it may be *felt*.

O confider well of it, (you the Subjects of this Kingdome) and rouze up your felves at length, in the behalf of your Soveraign and of your felves : remember the Honour and dignity of your forefa-
thers,

thers, the wisdome and valour that made them so famous and so feared : O where, where is the Auncient Gallantry of this *Noble Nation?*where is that life & courage,that was wont to kindle and flame in Englifh-men,when they faw themfelves efteemed fimple; and contemned as bafe and vile ? what is it all dead and buried in fnow and cold Afhes ? fhall it be thought that no fparks of it are yet remaining in your natures ? will you fuffer fervants alwaies to rule over you ; to inflave and inthrall *both you and your King* ? awake for fhame (or elfe for ever worthy to be defpifed) and look about you, bethink (at length) what you have to do.

Was ever Nation fo gull'd as you have been ? fo orereach'd by Cheaters ? did ever any who caried in their breafts the fpirits of men, delight to be fo abufed by their fellows ? to be made fools,ufed like Affes, and fo accounted ? and will you affect it ? fhall they, who triumph over you, think you alwaies *Children without underftanding* ? furely had they not believed you,as full of *weakneffe* ftill, as themfelves are of *wickedneffe,* they would not with that boldneffe, have imagined to flam you off, with fo bafe a *Narrative* againft your Soveraigne ; as if thereby they had given a fatisfactory reafon to your *fimplicities,* for all thofe wrongs which they have done Him.

And what do they aime at hereby, but to make Him moft odious and contemptible, who of all men living deferves the greateft Reverence, Love and Honour ? and why do they this ? but to the end, that they might have fome colour to deftroy Him.

And *will you Crucifie your King* ? (faies *Pilate* to the people of the *Jews*) as if he had faid, what an unheard-of vilany will that be ? How doth the Curfe cleave to that Nation for that act unto this very day? fo may it not be faid to you (O people of *England*) will you murder your King? will you fuffer your moft pious and gracious King, after all thefe unfpeakable abufes, which He hath already indured (for your fakes) at the hands of your Servants, (or *Reprefentatives* as they call themfelves) to be deftroyed by them ? if you play the *Jewes,* you fhall be payed like Jewes, you and your Pofterity fhall grone under the *Curfe of God and man* for ever : *qui non vetat peccare cum poteft, jubet ;* not to prevent a mifchief when you may, is directly to command it to be done.

As *Abfolom* by going in to his Fathers Concubines, on the houfetop, declared in the sight of all *Israel*, that He meant the breach should be irreconcielable, betwixt his Father and him : so have *these men*, by this their *Declaration* spoken loudly to all the world, that their intentions are, that the difference shall never be made up, betwixt their *Soveraign* and themselves : but (indeed) herein we may observe, that their impudence doth far exceed *Absoloms* : for while he was on *the house-top*, committing his wickednesse, he did not accuse the King his Father of the same sin, or lay heavily to his charge that very evill which himself was then in acting ; as *these men* have done ; for they in their *Declaration*, do burden their Soveraigne with their own faults; they tax Him of those very things which themselves have committed ; and that not only heretofore (when they were His ill Officers and Servants) but even now are acting at this very instant time before our faces, and upon our selves while they are exclaiming upon His Majesty.

And when should the King make Himself liable to all this blame and *odium* which they cast upon Him, was it since they promised to make Him so glorious? Themselves do not affirm this, but as they pretend a great while before : how comes it then to passe that in their present judgments, He who was formerly deemed fit to be made the *most glorious Prince in Christendome*, and promised so to be, (if He would but comply with them in those things that should be for His owne Honour and the Kingdomes good) is now in their present judgments (being still the same) become worthy of so much hatred as is here manifested, and not fit to have any more Addresses made unto Him ? bad are the memories of these men, the change of their condition hath made them quite forget their former principles and professions : what credit (think you) can be given henceforth unto them ? what n be put in any of their promises ? is it not likely they will fail you, (who ere you be that trust them) as they have done their Soveraigne ? nay, have they not failed you enough already ? do you look they will ever repay that Mony (with eight in the hundred interest) which they took up of you in *Publike Faiths* name ? what speciall respect do you observe, the City *London,* and the adjoyning Associate Counties do now find from them for all that wealth, countenance, and assistance which hath been afforded to them ? doe not they (like their owne father Satan)

tan) exact most still from those, whom they have found most
compliable, and most yeilding?

Nay more then this, do they not now discover a manifest adherence to the *schismaticall Army,* (which they intitle *the faithful Army*) against the City, the Associate Counties, the whole *Kingdome,* and *Scotland* too, as well as against the *King?* have not some of the unsavory *Aldermen,* Members of the *Commons'House,* gone senting up & down of late, and soliciting men to ingage themselves, *to live and die with the Parliament, and the Army?* and against whom? but *King and Kingdome,* who it seems are now looked upon, as one again, and conjoyned (though it be in the notion of Common Enemies) by these good Counsellours, these faithfull Representatives, that broke the friendly union. And what doth this new Ingagement speak unto you? but that their intentions are to rule from henceforth by the Sword; & without all Law, (save that of war) to keep you under. You may remember at first, 'twas *King and Parliament* they cried up, then *Parliament and Kingdome,* but now at length 'tis come to be *the Parliament and the Army* : so that you see how unsetled they are; how *God hath made them like to a wheel* in continuall motion, and therefore no confidence is to be put in them.

They promise now that *they will setle the Kingdome without the King;* who unsetled it but themselves? and for what cause did they so, but that themselves might reigne over us? and will they lay down their Rule, Authority and Power? surely no; and yet this they must be forced to do before the Kingdome will ere be setled. But how will they settle this Kingdom without the King? even as they have setled *Ireland:* they would never be quiet (as you all know) till the management of the war there (which themselves also (as is now believed) had an hand in raising,) might be wholly in their hands, with exclusion of His Majesty, (whom God hath appointed:) and too many of you the people (in the simplicity of your spirits) were for them against your Soveraign; and desired that the Parliament without the King might take order for that *Businesse,* and now you understand too plainly how well they have *ordered* the same, these two last years in speciall (while they had nothing else to mind, and have kept so many lazy Officers and Souldiers to burden and oppresse you.) O how do the poor neglected and straved Soldiery in that lost Kingdom, as well as the ruinated Protestants there, pour forth now their deserved *execrations*, and *curses* against these deceitfull and false-hearted men ! How are they now brought to beleeve and forced to confesse, that *none is, nor was, so tenderly affected towards them as the King*, and that Gods blessing will not concur with any endeavours there, till they be managed againe by Him, whom God hath intrusted ! O *remember Ireland, remember Ireland,* Happy may you be yet once againe in this Kingdom, if the miseries which have been felt in that, (since *these new Masters* tooke upon them to be the sole disposers of affaires there) may make you wary ; O take heed therefore in due time you do not beleeve them, when they say, *they will settle the Peace of this Kingdom without the King.*

Againe, they promised *to set up Jesus Christ in the Throne of his Kingdome,* but they meant themselves onely in the Throne of *this* : for do you not see how they have gone about it, and how far they have advanc'd their worke in 7. years ? Have they not imprisoned & turned out of Gods *Vineyard* the most faithfull and painfull *Labourers* ; forbidden them to preach in that name ; or to publish that truth which this Church professeth, and themselves protested to maintaine ? How many Congregations at this present want Pastors in this famous City ? and how many thousand Parishes are destitute in the Countries of right teaching ? now for what cause is all this ? why are Gods Prophets thus knocked off from their imployments ? wherefore are they inhibited the doing of their duties ? is it for any thing else, then because they inveigh against that wickednesse which God abhorreth ? are they not for this sole reason said to be enemies to the Parliament & to preach against that ? why do they not say in plaine termes, the *Parliament cannot sin* ? or that *sin* and *that* are all one, and must not be reproved ? or else (having nothing else to lay to their charge) why do not they suffer Gods Messengers to declare their Ambassage ? or if they will not so, let them (at least) discover themselves as openly in this, as they have done in other particulars ; for though they said as first, they tooke up Armes to *remove ill Councellors, and to bring Delinquents to punishment* ; yet now they can speake out and say, it was *to wrest the Legislative power and Militia*

tia out of His Majesties Hand: and though they promised at first to make the King Most Glorious, yet now they blush not to proclaime *we will not have this man to reigne over us, we will make no more addresses to Him,* we will exercise Authority *without Him and against Him.* So, though they promised at first *to set up Christ in His Throne,* let them now tell us in plaine English also, that *they meane to thrust Him,* and all that truely professe Him (according to the right Doctrine of the Gospel) *out of this Land,* for this is the very language of all their Actions.

Againe, they pretended great Emnity unto *Popish Doctrines and Tenents*; and Episcopacy was pull'd down out of zeale against *Popery,* (as if that had been a friend unto it.) With what clamours did they represent unto the people *Secretary Windebanks* intercourse with *Jesuites,* and *Popish Priests*; and the *Bishops* Chaplaines licencing of Books, supposed to be Popish; and yet these very men have permitted *Mabbot* (the allowed Broaker of all these venemous scriblings) to Authorize the Printing a booke of *Parsons* the *Jesuite,* full of the most *Popish* and *Treasonable positions* that were ever vented, for very good Doctrine; nay more then this, have they not contributed 30.l. toward the charge of Printing the same? & when (after its publication) it was told them by some, that the *said booke had been condemned by Parliament in the 35. of Queen* Elizabeth, *and that the Printer thereof was Hang'd, drawne, and quarter'd for the same; & that it was then enacted, that whosoever should have it in their house, should be guilty of high Treason,* when all this was related to some of the *Committee of Examinations,* did they not stop their eares at it? did they not slight those that thus spake unto them? their owne Consciences know all this to be true; and that we are able to prove it before the World; yet these be the men (forsooth) that hate Popery.

This *Popish Booke* (which we speake of) was at first published *Anno* 1524. under the name of *Dolman,* and intituled *a conference about the succession of the Crowne,* it consists of two parts, whereof the first conteines a *discourse of a Civill Lawyer, How and in what manner propinquity of blood is to be preferred:* it is divided into 9 Chapters: all which this *blessed Reforming Parliament,* hath now published under the Title of *Severall speeches delivered at a conference concerning the power of Parliaments, to proceed against*

R 3 *their*

their King, for misgovernment : they were all Answered (as they are in the *Jesuites* booke) by Sir *John Haward.Docter of the Civill Law* in the year 1603. and Dedicated to *King James* (which Answer is common in Booksellers shops to be still sold.

Now there is no difference, betwixt *this book* published by *this* Parliament, and that of the *Jesuite* condemned by *that other*, An. 35 . *Eliz.* but onely this : when the *Jesuite* mentions the Apostles, He addes the word Saint to their names S. *John*, S. *James*, S. *Peter*, which the Author of this new Edition leaves out, and saies plaine *John*, *James*, and *Peter* : and perhaps in some places the word *Parliament* is put in stead of the word *Pope*; or *people :* nay the variation is so little that it speakes the publisher. a very weake man, and those that set him on work none of the *wisest* in imploying so *simple an Animall*, in a businesse of so great concernment : we shall instance but in one passage.

Old *Dolman* or *Parsons* had said in the year 1594. that *many were then living in England, who had seen the severall Coronations of King* Edw. the 6. *Queen* Mary, *and Queen* Eliz. *and could witnesse*, &c. Now our *young Dolman* or *Walker* (for that is the wisemans name) supposing that all those people, were alive still that were old men 54. yeers agoe, like a true *Transcriber*, without the variation of a letter, affirmes it confidently, (in pag. 43. of his Edition) that *many are yet living in England, that have seen the severall Coronations of King* Edw. the 6. *Queen* Mary, *and Queen* Eliz. (to which he also addeth) King James *and King* Charls (because they were crowned since) and this we confesse is new in him.

Now by this very booke alone (though much more we might say to this purpose) tis very evident, that these Children of *Abaddon* love the *Jesuites Doctrine* well enough, so it comes not out in the *Jesuites owne name*, if it be but authorized by themselves or those appointed to publish and Licence books for the Parliament: O then 'tis very excellent good and Orthodoxall.

And now shall not these doings so palpably vile and grosse inflame your spirits (O English-men) and quicken you up to free your selves from their thraldome who thus abuse you ? will you suffer them still to proceed till they have stubbed up and quite o'rthrowne Christianity, from among you ? you now see plainly
enough

enough, what they meant at firſt by *Roote and branch* : it was not Epiſcopacy only *Roote and branch :* but Monarchy alſo *Roote and branch* ; the King and his Poſterity *Roote and branch,* the Nobility and Ancient Gentry *Roote and branch.* Peace and proſperity, honeſty and Loyalty, *Roote and branch,* with Proteſtant profeſſion it ſelfe, and all that good is, which in your *Proteſtation* generall you vowed to maintaine ; 'tis fit you ſhould obſerve it, All the particulars in the ſaid *Proteſtation* ſave onely one, are already averted and welnigh deſtroyed : the *Religion and worſhip of Chriſt eſtabliſhed in the Engliſh Church,* how is that ſuppreſſed and perſecuted ? His *Majeſties Perſon, Honour and Eſtate,* how are they abuſed, blaſted and imbezelled ? the *Priviledges of Parliament, Laws of the Land and Liberties of the Subject* ; how notoriouſly have they been infringed, violated, and overthrowne ? there remaines now but one particular to finiſh the whole worke of plucking up, or aboliſhing the Proteſtation *Roote and branch,* and that is *breaking the union betwixt the two Kingdomes of England and Scotland,* which now alſo they are indeavouring to effect, as appears ſufficiently by their unfriendly, nay *reproachfull Declaration* againſt the *Scotch Commiſſioners* and indeed againſt the whole Nation : and no queſtion but they will (if they can) force many of thoſe (whom they have made to ſweare the contrary) to joyne with them in this *breach* alſo, as they have done in all the former : if the *Scots* once begin to make conſcience of their old *oath of Allegeance;* and talke of their duty to their *Soveraigne Lord the King, His Crowne, and Dignity* ; of ſupporting His Power and Greatneſſe, according as they are bound by all Laws of God and nature ; then *away with theſe fellows from the earth* (cry thoſe that reſolve to make no more Addreſſes to the King) *'tis not fitting they ſhould live* ; though they were our *dear Brethren* before, yet now they are ſo no more, but *Malignants* as well as other folks, and fit for nothing but to have ſcorns, obloquies, and contempts caſt upon them.

And here (by the way) let the *Scottiſh Nation* obſerve it well, and they ſhall find upon tryall, that thoſe *Loyall Engliſh,* who from the beginning have adhered to their King, out of Conſcience and Allegiance, will be more carefull by all loving and friendly offices, to preſerve *peace,* and *unity,* betwixt the two Nations, from that *Common bond* of Chriſtianity and humanity.

which,

which ties us all together, then those others are, or will ever be, who have taken so many new Oaths, and Covenants to that purpose; all which, as they are unwarrantable, (wanting Legality and life from the Soveraign) so will they prove invalid, and too weak, to hold those who have ventured on them : nor were they intended (by those State-engineers who first devised them) as *Hen. Martin* tells the world, *to bind the takers everlastingly to each other*, or (indeed) to any other end, then to drive on present designes, and to batter the Consciences and souls of poor men ; who are ingaged by them (in very deed) to nothing else but to Repentance.

But we return to those of our *own Nation*, who now (we think) have fully seen the aymes, scopes, and endeavours of these miscreant persons, that have slighted all their Oaths, broken all parts of their Protestation, and are guilty of all the crimes that can be named from the highest Treason to the lowest Trespasse ; what is now therefore to be done by you, of this Anciently-noble *English* Nation, but to stand up for your *Religion, Laws*, and *Liberties*, to free your selves and Country from the insupportable Tyranny of these usurpers : to bring these superlative *Delinquents* to condigne punishment ; to endeavour speedily your Soveraignes restoration to His Dignity ; and to venture your lives, like good Christians and Gallant men, to deliver Him, that so many years protected and defended you, and hath now undergone (for your sakes) such *unparalleld sufferings* as nothing is superiour unto, but His *incomparable vertues*, and which (alas!) so many of you, have ignorantly, (by the fraudulent suggestion of these perfidious men) helped to bring upon Him ?

Be you assured, that all those *Arguments* and *Reasons*, which they falsely urged to stir you up to combine with them against him, are onely good and to be lawfully thought upon, to perswade you, to associate now against them. Had the King been truely taxable of that they charged on Him ; yet *Gods word, Christian verity*, and *the Law of the Land* forbids Resistance : but they all command the same against such as *these*, (though they were quite free from those other villanies which they abound in :) even because they are *usurpers* : for there is a vast difference between *usurpers* of Authority, and *ill managers* of lawfull Authority ; betwixt

twixt thoſe that *take power* to themſelves to doe miſchiefe with it, and thoſe that *exerciſe evilly* that lawfull power entruſted to them. Our Saviour (in the dayes of his fleſh) would not ſo much as cenſure *Pilate* for his cruell and bloody act, upon the *Galileans,* (when ſome did tempt him to it) that he might not ſeeme to countenance any, in ſo much as ſpeaking evilly of lawful power & authority, though abuſed. People when oppreſſed and wronged by their lawfull Superiour, have allowance onely *to cry unto God,* (as 1 *Sam.*8.18.) and to ſue for reliefe by way of Petition, as the *Iſraelites* in *Egypt* did to *Pharaoh,* when they were ſo cruelly uſed by his *Task-maſters.* But tis otherwiſe, if men be *uſurpers,* and ſet up themſelves, as *Abimelech* the *Bramble* did *Judg.*9. or endeavour to deſtroy the Royall Family, as *Athaliah* did : if they oppreſſe, (or whether they oppreſſe or no) all men are bonnd to riſe up againſt them, and to help that Royall Perſon or Family to their right, that ſuffers wrong by them ; for *fiat Juſtitia aut ruet mundus,* if Juſtice be not done in ſuch a caſe, the whole world it ſelfe (as may appear by the preſent temper of this Kingdome) will fall to ruine preſently.

As in a *Family,* if the *Maſter* or *Father* abuſe his Authority ; no *Child* or *Servant* of right, can lift up an Hand againſt him ; but if a *Child* or *Servant* ſhall take upon him to domineere over all his fellowes, and to abuſe his *Parent* or *Maſter,* all the reſt ought (and will if wiſe) riſe up againſt him, and help their oppreſſed Governour to his power and place again : So 'tis, and doubt-leſſe ſo it ought to be in a *Kingdome.*

A Kings ill uſage or reſtraint, is a full warrant and commiſſion to all His Subjects, to Arme themſelves for His liberty and reſtoration ; the power is never in the peoples hand, ſave in ſuch a caſe: but then they are all to advance as one man, in the behalf of their common Father ; and to take thoſe lawleſſe *Wolves* and *Beares* (they are *Buchanans* words) who have no more right of authority over any, without their Soveraignes leave, (much leſſe over Himſelfe) then *vermine* have (ſuch as *Weaſels* and *Polcats* are) over Hens and Chickens ; yea and untill the people doe ſo riſe, they are (undoubtedly) not onely under the uſurpers danger, but alſo under Gods heavy curſe.

Curſe ye Meroz (ſaid the Angel of the Lord) curſe ye with a
bitter

bitter curse *the inhabitants thereof, because they came* not to help the *Lord, i. e.* the Captaine of the Lord , the Anointed of the Lord, the Supreme Judge and Magistrate under the Lord *against the mighty*, that is, against those sturdy and rebellious *Canaanites,* who were growne so mighty, (by that strength of *Militia,* and *Chariots of Iron* which they had gotten) and did so *mightily oppresse* Israel, under whom they ought to have lived in obedience.

That Scripture (you all know) hath been much used of late, and as much abused ; but tis never truly applyable save in such a case as this in present is : for the *Captaine of the Lord* is now in as much, yea in more distresse, then at that time ; His *people* under as great oppressions ; and the enemies as very *Canaanites* as those were, as much the *children of Malediction,* if not more ; for those were under the curse partly for *Cham* their fathers sin , but these are solely for their owne ; which hath been not onely of the same kind, as His was, (mocking and scorning at their Father) but acted with more impudency and vilenesse a great deale; for *Cham* found his father *naked,* but these have endeavoured (by this their cursed Declaration, & many others of like sort) to make theirs appear so; yea they have proclaimed him *naked* when he was not; in a most shamelesse manner they have shewn their *owne nakednesse,* & then published it to be their Fathers ; and that not only to their *Brethren* (as He did) whose piety and modesty was apt to *hide* and *cover the same,* (whose ere it was) but to the whole world, to strangers, to enemies, that would be ready to credit the same, and glad to divulge it farther to their Fathers defamation ; which was the very thing they aimed at : therefore *these* evill workers are more the *people of Gods curse,* then those *Canaanites* were ; nor had those provoked Gods wrath (so much as these have done) by their breaches of so many *oathes* and *protestations,* of Loyalty and Obedience ; nor had they practiced more injustice and oppression ; therefore if *they* were designed to be subdued, and pulled downe from their usurped greatnesse ; much rather may we beleeve that *these* are; and if *Meroz* was lyable to so sharp a doome, for not *helping the Lord* against *them,* then well may we feare a like portion, if we be backward in our assistance to the downfall of *these* men.

For are not these Gods enemies as well as any ? nay more then any ?

any? Did *true Religion* ever receive such difgrace and fcandall as thefe have offered to it? Did this famous Kingdom ever produce fuch *monfters of Nature* before now? Surely the Kings of the earth, and the Inhabitants of the world would never have belieued (if thefe had not been to evidence the fame) that the *Englifh Nation* could ever have bred fuch *Vipers*; or that among *Proteftant Chriftians* there fhould poffibly have been fuch *Malignant adverfaries unto Piety and Princes.*

Take courage therefore you may againft them, (all ye who in Chrifts name, and the Kings behalfe fhall oppofe them:) for their high and great wickedneffe againft God, fpeaks them out of his protection; as alfo doth their confidence in the *Arme of flefh.* For in very deed they *make not God their ftrength* (what ever is pretented;) nor ever did, but the *Militia* rather, for which they have contefted: that is their Magazine of Hope, and Tower of Safety: their truft is, and hath been in the multitude of their Weapons, their Armies of Men, their numerous Affociations, and their plenty of ill gotten Riches, wherewith they have, and think ftill to bribe and buy off thofe, whom by force and power they cannot mafter.

And thefe be the *fparkes* which they have *kindled, and compaffe themfelves about* withall: Thefe be the very *fires* they rejoyce in, the *ftayes* they reft upon, but fayes the Lord to fuch as they are, that do as they do; *This fhall ye have of my Hand, ye fhall lie down in forrow,* Ifay 50. 11.

And do we not daily fee *the things that are comming upon them, making hafte?* Are not their Hearts unjoynted from one another? Is not their *Kingdome divided,* their Affociations broken? Are not they that were *girded* fafteft to them, fallen from them? How loudly do all perfons every where cry out upon them? How generally odious are *they* become of late, who were before fo much adored? How much greater now among all men is the *Hatred* of them then the *fear*? Who lookes not upon them as *the people of Gods Curfe*? as the very *poyfon* and *peftes* of the Kingdome? who beleeves not that divine vengeance hangs over the Land, while they walke at liberty in it? fee, fee and confider it well; how *fpider*-like they have been catch'd in their own *nets, and fnared in the work of their own Hands;* How have they befooled themfelves

in

in their owne-doings ; How-hath their scandalous *Declaration* against the King raised plenty of fewd in mens hearts against themselves ? hath not all their filthy fome spit out therein against Him, flew wholly back into their owne faces ? is not His Majesty become thereby more deare and precious to His people, and themselves far more detestable ? are their solemne *Orders* or *Ordinances*, entertained with any more respect now, then scorne it selfe can afford them ? do not most men as slightly receive whatever comes from them, as themselves have done the Kings Messages ?

And whence now is all this ? who hath effected and brought to passe these things ? hath not the Lord ? and do they not plainly speake the approaching end of these men, or of their greatnesse and prosperity ? are not all these particulars, so many evident prognosticks of their ruine ? and may they not be taken too, as so many invitations from God, to rouze up our selves against them, and as so many intimations of His concurrence with us in such endeavours? nay, and 'tis to be noted too, when the Almighty (for our encouragement and hope) did begin thus to worke, it was at such a time, as these usurpers were at their greatest height, when they cryed out with open mouth *who is Lord over us ? ours is the power and we will prevaile.* When they had resolved to make *no more Addresses to the King,* but to do as themselves pleased, *without Him and against Him.* Then, then did our God *awake as one out of sleepe* ; then did he set himselfe against these men to confound them in their wayes, and to expose them to this publike contempt and scorne of all ; And 'tis Gods course if he once begins, not to leave off, till he hath made an end too, *Root and branch* in a short time ; the *spirit* saies it, *branch and rush in one day.*

Indeed the Lord hath been fitting them for their shame a great while ; He hath left them to themselves *because they regarded not to know God,* or to please him ; He hath given them up to a *reprobate sense* (as a punishment for their sin) not to take notice of his hand going out against them, threatning ruine and extirpation of them : yea he hath *blinded their eyes, & hardned their hearts* to forsake their *owne mercy* : He infatuated their spirits to loose those oportunities so frequently offered, and to despise the profers of peace so often tendred, whereby they might have been secured.

Now

Now as pride goes before deſtruction, ſo folly (we know) preceedes a fall.

Undoubtedly the Lords purpoſe is, to make them the aſtoniſh-ment of the world for *confuſion* and *miſery*, as they have made themſelves the amazement of the world for *wickedneſs* and *impie-ty* : He will bring upon them, all the *blood* which they have ſhed, all the *guilt* thereof, and ſo of all the *blaſphemies* which they have vented,he ſhall make them *vomit up again* all the wealth of others which they have ſwallowed , *according to their ſubſtance ſhall the reſtitution be :* for *ſhall not the Judge of all the earth* (when he takes the matter into his owne hand) *doe righteouſly ?* never a perſecu-tor or oppreſſor, never an Apoſtate or falſe Traytor, never a Parliament *Sheba*, or Pulpit-*Shimei* of them all, but ſhall meet with his due demerit from him who hath pronounced of them, or of ſuch as they be ; that *they ſhall lie downe in ſorrow.*

And thus you ſee what hopes there be of your ſpeedy delive-rance, (O ye miſerably oppreſſed *Engliſh*) if you will now ariſe as one man, and ſhew your ſelves :. you ſee how God is already gone out againſt your enemies, How his *Juſtice* is ingaged for you, and doth march before, to invite you to follow after. And if you looke but on the other ſide, you may ſee his *mercy* as mani-feſtly appearing for your further incouragement. How hath that gracious Prince (whoſe ſervants you are) not ſlaine, but *Conquered his thouſand,* his *ten thouſand,* yea his *hundred thouſand* of hearts and men ? and that not with *ſword* or *ſpeare,* or any inſtrument of war ; but by the ſole ſtrength of Gods mighty ſpirit, animating his ſoul in his great Afflictions, and carrying him on high, *above: the waters.* How hath He like the glorious Sun, by the bright luſture of His Graces, broake through all thoſe black clouds of calumny and ſlander, whereby theſe enemies of Majeſty have la-boured to obſcure Him ? How hath He by his wiſdome, meeke-neſſe, patience, and conſtant tenders of mercy to His greateſt ene-mies recovered, yea and overcome (as Chriſt himſelf did) the minds and affections of His people ? How hath his miſeries for their ſakes turned the ſtreames of their love towards Him ? ſure-ly *this is the Lords doing*; the victory is welnigh already won for us, by Gods ſole ſtrength in the Perſon of our Soveraigne.

How doth their black mouth'd *Balaams,* who for the *wages of*

iniquity

iniquity have spit out so much *venome* against His Majesty, (whom they never had more knowledge of, then was brought unto them by His deadly enemies,) How do they now even *gnash* their teeth, and *gnaw* their tongues for sorrow ; to here how His *vertues* are admired, and His *graces* reverenc'd : to feele how His *splendour* hath darkned them, by causing their vilenesse to appear, in dissipating the slanders and dissolving the filth, which (with so much paines and pulpit sweat) they had laboured to bespatter him with, seven years together.

And now ; are not these most evident markes of Gods *favour* to the King, and that His *mercies* are also ingaged on His side, as well as His *Justice*, and will be on yours if you are for Him ? 'Tis true; God hath seem'd to sleep long to the cause of His Anointed, that the incredible and high wickednesse of the enemy might be known ; and the invisible or inward excellencies of the King seen ; but both these ends being now accomplished, the time is fully come of *Gods arising*, which will be the indoubted cause of His *enemies scattering*.

What (therefore) doth now remaine for you to do (O *English* people) but to make haste in the first place, to fetch back your King to His Throne and Dignity, in despight of those that keep Him Prisoner : See, see how the Ancient *Britaines* move already : nay, see how the *Scots* do promise to appear : Have not you cause to thinke that they intend to plead with you, (as *Judah* did with *Israel,*) for the Honour of the worke ; *because the King is neer of kin to them ?* but have not you *ten parts in Him*, and so more right in this *David* now, then they, and reason to be as early in view unto this service ? assuredly, though we gave the *Scots* leave to be the first, in departing from duty ; yet we should all blush, not to be (at least) as forward as they, in returning to it : nay, we should all like good Christians, and penitent men, contend in love both with them, and one another, who shall be the formost.

And then let us all as one man conjoyne in this ; to require of our false *Stewards* a present *account of their stewardships* : let's resolve upon it, that they shall no longer be stewards for us, because they have made such *waste of our goods*; and of what ever else was dear unto us ; and if they refuse to come to an account at such

our

our call, let's force them to it ; full fore fhall we fin againft God, and the whole Kingdome, if we ftill permit them in their places : we can doe no wrong in bringing them to a Legall triall, (which is the thing we muft aime at:) if they have (as they fay) *defended the Law*, no doubt but *the Law will defend them* : but if they have broaken or laboured to deftroy that, (which they pretended to maintaine, and were intrufted by us fo to doe) 'tis but juft and right, that they by it fhould be corrected.

And the difturbers of our peace being taken down or removed from us ; let's then call to minde that we are all of the fame Nation, and were partakers of the fame Baptifme ; and therefore ought to lay afide that which *preffeth down*, or hardneth our Hearts againft one another, to put away what ever hindreth from clofing together in affections : it may fuffice that we have played the fools hitherto, gone aftray and quarrell'd all this while for we know not what : we muft now *remember whence we have fallen*, and *return to our firft Love*, to our bounden duty : our Soveraign like the *Prodigalls Father*, (as appears by his many *gratious Meffages*) is inclined to receive us ; the Church like a tender hearted Mother, (*that cannot forget the children of her wombe*) will (upon our repentance) be ready to pardon us, and to folicite our Heavenly Father for us. Thofe that have fuffered wrong muft be difpofed to forgive ; thofe that have done wrong muft be willing to reftore what they have unjuftly feized upon ; that fo all impediments to Heaven, and Peace may be removed, and we no more return to folly.

And laftly, that there may be a well *grounded peace* indeed, betwixt the *two Nations of England* and *Scotland* ; and that we may live together, as Brethren ought to doe : let thofe of that *Kirk*, who are yet fo zealous for their *Covenant*, that they would have it forc'd upon their Soverain, & the people of this Kingdom, (as if it were the very foundation of Chriftian Religion, and as neceffary as the Gofpel it felfe:) Let them be pleafed to confider calmely and ferioufly, how little of Gods bleffing both they and we have had, fince the firft birth of it : how the *Reformation* (fo much talked on) hath been obftructed : How the *Proteftant profeffion* formerly planted hath been defaced : How the *Enemy of that and mankinde* hath fowen the *tares* of falfe Doctrine, fince

(to

(to promote the Covenant) so many of the Clergy, have omitted to walke in those wayes of peace, humility, and obedience which Gods word prescribeth; How much contention and bloodshed hath been caused, how many Sects and Heresies have sprung up, How much blasphemy hath been vented, what strange perverseness of spirit, and unreverent language hath been used against Soveraigne Majesty, what little manners hath been shewne unto superiors, what occasions sought to quarrel with them, what catching at their words, what wresting and misinterpreting of their writings and sayings, and all (as hath appeared) out of zeal unto the *Covenant.* O that they would please to consider of these things; and withall to remember that *Christianity* commands *morality* and to give to every men his due, *fear to whom fear,* and *honour to whom honour belongeth* ; it requires singlenesse of heart, & injoynes to us deny our selves to please others, that they would hereupon desist to pursue with such heat their owne fancy, they knowing it to be point-blanke against an Act of their Parliament, 1585. *(which utterly prohibits all Leagues, Covenants, or bands whatsoever, without the Kings consent.* And that they would also take notice, how inconsistent their said *Covenant* is, with the constitution and temper of this our Kingdome : How 'tis not only broken, but derided, and scorned at now by many of those, who were at first very *furious* for it. In a word, that they would beleeve the *English Nation* in generall, doth as little like of what is put upon them by the *Scots,* as the *Scots* did, of what was sent unto them from the *English* ; to speake plainly and truely, we have generally as little affection to their *Covenant,* as they had (when time was) to our *Booke of Common-Prayer,* and shall as ill digest it.

Nor indeed are the *English* Nobility and Gentry so weake spirited, as those of *Scotland* may appear to be, in letting their Clergy, (the chief promoters of the Covenant) under pretence of that to *act the Pope* among them ; by obstructing the progresse of Civill affaires, and meddling in State matters. Should our Churchmen (as those there have lately done) put in bars against the Kings settling , or say that *themselves must have satisfaction before the King be restored to the exercise of His Regall power :* with what disdaine would our right Nobility, and true Gentry,

(yea

(yea and well inftructed Commonalty too) receive the fame; they would reply upon them in this fort, and fay: what warrant have you from Gods word to fpeake after this manner? you that fhould by your office and Miniftry be teachers and patterns to all, of humility and obedience, will you Lord it, and that not onely over Gods flock, but over his Shepheard too, his Supreame of all? muft not He injoy His owne right, His place, His Inheritance, nor exercife that power which God hath committed to Him, without your leave? much leffe fhall any of us fhortly (that are inferiour to Him) command over our owne poffeffions without your allowance if we liften to you in this thing: furely, *you take too much upon you, ye fons of Levi:* they are the *Kings of the Earth* (faies your Mafter Chrift) that are to *exercife Authority* over men, and (by your favour) over the Clergy too; and not the Clergy over Kings: if you are for that fport, goe pack to *Rome* among your fellows.

Thus fhould we in *England* be anfwered, and put off, with due rebukes, if we fhould be fo drawne away from Scripture and from duty by a *Scotifh* Covenant: And therefore it would be good, if thofe in that Kingdome, who are ftill fuch *zelots* for it; would pleafe in coole blood to confider of it; and (according to the Apoftles councell) *ftudy quietneffe, minde their owne bufineffe:* and as *Solomon* advifeth, *leane no more to their owne underftanding,* Idolize no longer their own *devices,* prefs no further their own *inventions:* rather let them and we (as becomes *members* of one Chrift, and *Subjects* of one King) conjoyne firft in reftoring our Soveraigne to His Throne and power: and then in begging of Him, that a *Generall Councell* or Affembly may be call'd, of the moft *Learned, peaceable,* and *grave* men in all his Kingdomes: to argue with meekneffe (as becomes the Gofpel) the *cafes of difference* that are amongft us: And to their *determinations* (ratified by the King,) let us all fubmit with ready hearts and humble minds: So fhall the luftre and Honour of our *Proteftant profeffion* be recovered, which (by thefe unhappy jars) hath been defaced: the *peace* of many Confciences fhall be fetled; *Sects, Herefies,* and *Falfe Doctrines* fhall be fuppreffed; *tranquility, light,* and *love* fhall be again reftored to the people of both Nations;

T   And

And *we,* (if we are the *happy instruments* of this,) shall hereby increase our *Comfort, Crowne* and *Glory.*

Now the *God of all Grace,* poure upon us all his *Spirit of Grace,* to worke up our *Spirits* to an holy frame, and Chrstian temper. Amen. Amen.

FINIS.

Lightning Source UK Ltd.
Milton Keynes UK
UKHW021234241118
332794UK00012B/1881/P

9 780483 002913